The COMPLETE Book of

KARATE

& SELF DEFENSE

Formerly
THE COMPLETE BOOK OF SELF DEFENSE

Compiled by Robert V. Masters

STERLING PUBLISHING CO., INC.　**NEW YORK**

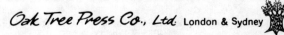

Oak Tree Press Co., Ltd. London & Sydney

Contents

PART I

body-
building and
self-defense

Throughout this building-up routine, you will learn how to make your muscles work for you and how to take advantage of every movement of your body. You'll find yourself unconsciously exercising even as you read.

1. A Sound Body

Studies at Yale University, the United States' Military Academy at West Point, and the University of Illinois have proved that the physical fitness of Americans is in a state of "gradual deterioration." We are "not nearly as fit" as young people in Great Britain or Japan. In fact, many British girls are physically superior to American boys in the ten-to-thirteen age group.

Most people aren't physically fit—including a lot of athletes. A few years ago a research organization, called Sports College, made a very interesting study of 2,700 athletes engaged in all kinds of sports. Not one of them did better than 65% of his possible peak performance. Almost all were below par in strength, speed, and endurance; almost all were weak in arm and shoulder strength.

Here is an example: A physically fit person should certainly be able to do twenty-five two-hand push-ups without great strain. Yet only one in seventeen of the athletes tested could do that. Only one in seventy-four of them could do a single one-arm push-up—admittedly a much more difficult feat. Only one in eighty-two could do a single one-arm pull-up on a chinning bar. While they're not as good as they should be, the athletes obviously are in better shape than the rest of us. How do *you* stack up? How many push-ups can you do? How many pull-ups? How long can you run without getting winded?

Body-building exercises and self-defense training activities probably appeal most to boys and young men from the ages of 10 to 25; but *anyone* can benefit greatly from this kind of exercise, if it is approached sensibly. At least from the viewpoint of physical fitness, the 10-to-25 group is, ironically, the group that needs this book least. In terms of strength, speed, endurance, and general fitness, the peak years are reached at 17 to 19, and the peak in physical condition continues for the next 7 to 9 years. Physically, these are your best years. This is the time to take advantage of your abundant energy and high muscle tone. Physiologically, "middle age" begins at 26. At this time your physical condition begins to gradually decline. Thus, the 30-year-old man needs physical training even more than his 15-year-old brother.

You would not be reading this book if you were not conscious of your body. Your physical appearance and your muscular growth are important to you—as they should be. You want to look well, feel well, and perform well.

You have seen and admired the excellent physiques of others—friends, athletes, weight-lifters, gymnasts—and want your own physical appearance to be as good. You want to be proud of your body, not ashamed of it or self-conscious about it. Nobody wants to be skinny, or fat; every healthy boy and adult man wants to be solid, strong, and confident.

But I hope you believe, as the Roman poet Juvenal believed, two thousand years ago, in "a sound mind in a sound body." For this is not a book for muscle-heads. The guy who is nothing but an athlete is certainly no better off than the guy who's nothing but a bookworm. Your goal, I hope, is to achieve a full and balanced life in both directions.

A great many boys and young men are dissatisfied with their

physical appearance, perhaps even embarrassed about their poor development. They lack confidence, especially in their ability to defend themselves. They may never have had a physical encounter; they may guiltily suspect that they're "cowards."

If you're not a bully, you should never have to suffer from those miserable feelings of guilt. Nobody is born a hero. Physical confidence and courage must be trained and developed.

I hope to show you how to build up your body. Even without training in self-defense, body-building will do a great deal for your physical and psychological well-being. People who are small, or at least not very strong, often enroll in judo classes because they've heard that size and strength don't necessarily matter. To a degree this is true. But you must become quite expert at any "gentle" art of self-defense before you can feel really confident.

Why should you accept weakness? You can't do much about being short, but there is plenty you can do about being weak. Learning to defend yourself is part of the answer; body-building is another part.

Maybe you're not physically unfit. You may be in excellent physical condition, active in sports, but you may be interested in doing more in the way of body-building and weight-lifting, or perhaps your primary interest is in training for self-defense.

Whatever your personal situation may be, this is a book for all boys and men who want to take pride in their physical development and develop confidence in their ability to face any situation.

This book is not intended to be an encyclopedia of body-building and self-defense techniques. There are many excellent books, both basic and advanced, on judo, scientific unarmed combat, body-building, and weight-training. This is a basic book for beginners of any age. It will take you some time to master even the simpler techniques, but they can do wonders for you. They will not make you a champion weight-lifter, ready for the Olympics; they will not qualify you for a black belt in judo. But give them a chance. Mastery of these methods—by means of regular training and practice—*can* give you enough self-confidence and ability to handle almost any situation you're likely to encounter. Faithful training with weights can give you the appearance and muscular power you want.

In short, this book is not the last word; but it can be much more than just a good beginning. That's up to you. The important thing is to start *now* to master these techniques; then, if you like, you'll be ready to go on to advanced work.

The book is divided into two main sections: one on body-building, one on self-defense. The first section is arranged in order of increasing difficulty: that is, an increasing amount of physical energy is required to perform the exercises as you progress.

Illus. 1: The hip throw, a basic judo technique.

Illus. 2: The alternate press with dumbbells.

Which exercises are right for you? That will depend on what condition you're in now, and what you'd like to accomplish. If you think you're in fairly good shape, you may want to start right in on the weight-lifting work. If, for any number of personal reasons, you're not ready for that yet, you may want to concentrate on the setting-up exercises. Or you may find that the next chapter is most appealing. It deals with a number of exercises that are casual, effective, and fun. It will put you in condition for more strenuous work or keep you trim even if you care to go no further in body-building.

In self-defense "difficulty" has a different meaning. It means the increasing degree of skill and practice necessary to master a technique. Although all the self-defense methods in this book are basic, considerable practice is still necessary to perfect any of them. So the section on self-defense is not arranged in any particular order. All that's required is that you and your partner *learn how to fall* before going on to the various throws.

It's possible, of course, to treat body-building and self-defense as separate activities. That's what many others have done. One fellow says, "So what if I'm not very strong? I can be good at judo!" And the other says, "So what if I don't know self-defense? Look how strong I am!"

You don't have to make a choice; you can try both. You'll go twice as far by thinking of body-building *and* self-defense as parts of a single goal: the goal of confident manhood. Each activity helps the other, and both combined help *you*. It's a tough combination to beat.

2. Muscles Can Be Fun

We've started off with a reasonable assumption: Most boys and men want to have good strong bodies. You feel better in every way when you know you're in good condition.

What does it take to get in condition? Expensive equipment? A gym? A lot of precious time? Hard work? Are you afraid of what other people might say? Would you be embarrassed to be caught lifting weights?

The facts are that body-building equipment isn't really expensive; you don't need a gym; you *do* have time; and it doesn't have to be hard work. It can be a lot of fun, whether you work by yourself or with a friend, or friends.

There are as many ways of developing your body as there are of moving your muscles. Doing exercises and calisthenics is one way; lifting weights is another. Participating in sports and athletic activities is a third. Self-defense training is yet another way—it helps you build up a strong, hard, flexible body.

But there's a fifth way to develop your body and have fun doing it. It doesn't involve setting-up exercises, or weight-lifting, or any special equipment, or regular workouts at a gym. It's the "casual" way to physical fitness. It won't give you a weight-lifter's body, but it can keep you in remarkably good shape. This method has been used and is still being used by some of the busiest, best-known people in America—movie and television stars, show-business people, athletes, corporation presidents.

What's more, you don't always need "the privacy of your own room," as the ads say. You can use this method, *unnoticed*, in the middle of a crowd. You can use it in a crowded elevator. Best of all, you don't have to set aside a special amount of time.

And now, what's the secret method? It involves two things: simple muscle tension and taking advantage of brief seconds and minutes throughout the day.

Suppose you're standing on a street corner, waiting for a bus You're holding a package in your left hand; your right arm is hanging down at your side. Make a tight fist with your right hand, and tense your forearm muscle. Bend your fist in and around and up toward your elbow; feel that forearm muscle flex. Keep it flexed for about six seconds, then release it.

That simple tension exercise, repeated just once a day for a couple of months, will produce a forearm muscle as hard as a board.

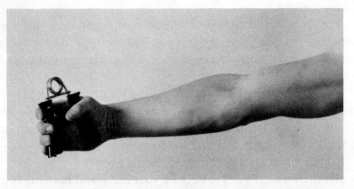

Illus. 3: Squeeze a hand-grip to develop the hand, wrist and forearm muscles.

This method of exercise is based on a new theory of muscle growth. German and American scientists and doctors have found

Illus. 4: The chest-expander also serves as a
biceps-builder.

that a muscle can grow at only a certain rate. And, according to
this theory, it doesn't take as much work as we used to think. If you
flex any muscle to its maximum power and contraction, and hold it
there for six seconds, once a day, the scientists say, the muscle
will grow in strength just as fast as it *can* grow.

Whether or not this method of muscle tension can ever really
replace weight-lifting is still a matter of controversy. Some
scientists say it can; endless repeating of strenuous exercise, they
say, "does not make the strength of a muscle grow any faster."
Weight-lifting, however, may make the *size* of the muscle grow
faster.

The new six-second theory is far from fully accepted in this country. But while it may or may not guarantee maximum growth, one thing is certain: it does bring an increase in muscular growth and strength.

If you're not ready or able to start a weight-lifting program, give this method a chance. Stay with it every day for a few months. Work on every muscle. Tighten your stomach for six seconds; push the abdominal muscles out as far as you can, then relax. Pull your stomach *in* for six seconds—all the way—hold it—let go. Do the same with your biceps; then with your triceps.

You flex the triceps by bringing your arms straight up in back of you as far as they can go. Or, hold a broomstick or a ruler behind your back, holding it with both hands. Now, keeping your arms

Illus. 5: Develop the triceps with a dowel or broomstick.

Illus. 6: Another way to strengthen back muscles.

straight, raise the stick or ruler as high as you can. Hold your arms there for six seconds—then release. If you've never done that before, you'll discover muscles you never knew you had.

The television star Hugh O'Brian (*Wyatt Earp*) uses casual muscle tension when he stands talking to someone. He presses the fist of one hand into the open palm of the other, putting tension on the muscles of both arms and shoulders. Other stars—Frankie Laine and Jane Powell, for example—also take advantage of brief seconds throughout the day. When they're sitting in their cars, waiting for traffic lights to change, they do the stomach exercises described above. Theodore Roosevelt, thin and weak as a boy, developed the habit of kneading and massaging his neck muscles during spare moments. It's a good practice to pick up; squeezing and pounding and massaging your own muscles will do a great deal to keep them firm and toned. The habit transformed Roosevelt's neck into a solid and powerful one.

Do you have to go to a gym to keep in shape? Not at all. Anybody who thinks he can't exercise because there are "no facilities around" just isn't using his imagination.

Illus. 7: Work out on rings to develop gymnastic ability.

When I was 14, I felt that my arms and shoulders were weak, and wanted to lift weights, but I was too self-conscious to admit it. I went down to a machine-metal shop and bought a short, 12-pound bar of steel, because it was inconspicuous and easy to hide.

I made up my own exercises, and I think I had as much fun with that steel bar as I would have had with a complete gym.

A few years later, I discovered that a friend of mine was doing the same thing. *His* "barbell" was a crankshaft from an old car. He had kept it in his bedroom for years, lifting it and working out for an hour or two every couple of days. He wasn't a husky guy—but his arms were like spring steel.

No matter where you live, you can always dig up something to throw around and lift. A bar of metal, a length of pipe—even a long-handled shovel—can serve as a light barbell when you're starting out. You may have to double or triple the number of repetitions, but you'll soon feel the weight.

Illus. 8: Exercise equipment is available at most sporting goods stores.

An old broomstick can do as much good for your hands and fingers as any training device in the world. Hold it by one end in either hand, so that it's hanging down. Then, using just your fingers and thumb, "walk down" the broomstick until your fingers have reached the other end. See how many times you can do *that* one—and then challenge your friends to try it. It's one of the best ways to develop strength in your fingers, hands, wrists, and forearms.

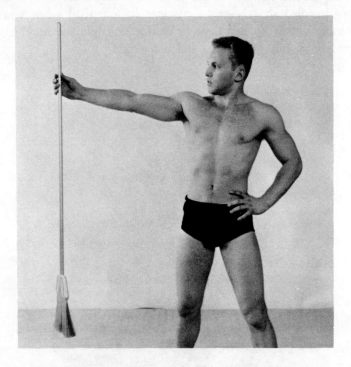

Illus. 9: Try "walking down" a broomstick with fingers and thumb.

If you're a football or soccer player and want to strengthen your neck muscles, try the pillow exercise. Place a pillow against the wall at your shoulder level, and push into it with your head from different positions. From the front, use the top of your head and forehead. Twist sideways and push with the sides of your head. Finally, turn around and push with the back of your head.

I remember reading of a college football coach who told one of his players to do that exercise. A few weeks later, the player came to him and said, "If I keep this up, I'm going to need new shirts." The coach laughed.

"Don't worry about it," he said. "Continue the exercise. I'll pay for the new shirts if you gain enough to need 'em. It's worth it." The coach finally did buy six new shirts for his athlete; the fellow increased his neck-width by two sizes.

Do you need stronger wrists or ankles? Do what the Army man does—rotation exercises. Rest your right leg on your left knee, and grasp your right ankle with your left hand. Then, describe a complete circle with your toes: first, counter-clockwise for forty rotations, then clockwise for another forty. Do the same with your left leg. But 80 a day with each ankle isn't enough—that's just four sets. You should do four sets three or four or five times a day to get real results. Does that sound like a lot? Soldiers with weak ankles did 10,000 a day!

The same kind of exercise—simple rotation—can be applied to strengthen the wrists; or you may prefer Peewee Reese's favorite exercise. Reese used to carry a rubber ball or tennis ball around with him, and squeeze it hundreds of times a day. Squeeze until your muscles are tired. Then take a 30-second break, and go at it again.

Can you climb a rope? It's a wonderful way to develop arm and shoulder strength, a strong grip, good stomach muscles. It's hard at first, then it gets easy; and when it's easy, it's fun. Keep trying every day. You don't need a gym: all you need is a good sturdy 20-foot length of rope, and a solid, live tree. The rope should be knotted securely to a branch at least 15 feet off the ground. The official height in Army and Navy guerilla training is 18 feet. If you want to get in shape for rope-climbing, practice your chinning. Learn how to lock your feet around the rope, so you can stop at

Illus. 10: Another hand-grip exerciser.

any point on the way up or down. You can come down slowly that way, so that the rope doesn't burn your hands.

And speaking of climbing—when was the last time you climbed a tree? Get your buddies outdoors, into the woods and fields. There's a world of activity waiting for you. See what the country-side looks like from 20 or 30 feet up; just make sure you can get down again.

Practice your jumping; build up the spring in your legs. Jump across streams and ditches. Jump to the side, and up in the air. Pull down a leaf from that branch that's just out of your reach—or is it? Practice your running and racing. Build up your legs and wind with dashes and cross-country jogs; try some imaginary broken-field running.

Play volleyball—it's a wonderful sport that develops and toughens your whole body. You have to be able to get up high in the air when you play the net, and spiking the ball develops good shoulders and back muscles. You have to twist and turn and bend and spring—all good for the abdominal and trunk muscles. You have to pass the ball accurately and set it up for a teammate to spike—good exercise for fingers and wrists.

If you want a sport that can be more fun (and often rougher) than football, and just as good for your leg muscles, try soccer. Anybody who thinks it's easy, just hasn't played. It's good for your breathing and wind and endurance, and the body contact takes as much courage and nerve as any sport in the world.

Work with a buddy about your own size and weight, and help each other toughen up. Indian arm- and leg-wrestling are good old standbys, and still a lot of fun. If you want to get in shape for the judo balance that's coming up later, practice the hand-pull. You and your partner clasp right hands, and stand with the outer side of your right feet touching. The object is to make the other fellow lose his balance completely, or lift his right foot off the ground, by using your wits in pushing and pulling.

Illus. 11: Compete with a partner in the hand-pull.

If you want to build up your biceps without lifting weights, try elbow-wrestling. Indoors, sit at a table, or lie prone on a rug, facing your partner. Outdoors, of course, you can lie on the grass. Clasp hands, then, resting your elbows on the table, move them together until they touch and are vertical; now try to force your partner's hand all the way down to the table or ground without moving your elbow.

One of the world's most famous body-builders did an interesting variation of this when he was a boy—and not a strong boy, at that. He got hold of a good, strong metal spring, and clamped it into a vise. Then he took a wooden dowel, or a sawed-off broomstick, and forced it down into the spring, leaving 6 or 8 inches protruding from the spring for a good grip. To build up his arms and shoulders, he practiced pushing, pulling, and bending the spring over as far as he could.

And now, I think you have the idea. Make up your own stunts. Use your imagination. Anything you do to put continued tension on a muscle is good body-building exercise. When you begin to see results, I think you'll agree that muscles can be fun.

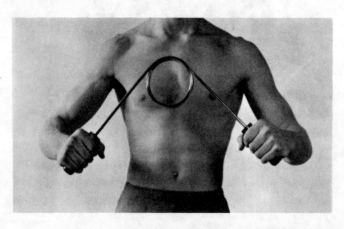

Illus. 12: A spring exerciser designed for beginners.

3. Tumbling

You may know how to do a headstand or a simple forward roll, but how about a handstand? Can you do a backward flip? A cartwheel? An Arabian somersault? These stunts are not only fun, but also wonderful exercise. Tumbling is a body-builder; it develops coordination, balance, agility, stamina—and muscle. If you become good at it, you'll be better prepared when you get to judo and the other forms of self-defense.

Tumbling is a sport all its own, of course, and this chapter describes only the basic tumbling skills—about ten of them. But if you master these, you'll be well on your way to advanced gymnastics. All you need to start with is a mat.

"If you master these" . . . it sounds easy. But don't let these brief descriptions fool you into thinking you can be an acrobat overnight. It's *not* easy. It takes time to master the basic skills—the headstands and handstands, backward and forward flips, cartwheels and handsprings.

The best way to learn, of course, is to get expert help—from an instructor or an accomplished gymnast. Most gym teachers know how to teach these basic techniques, or you might find willing instructors and classes in boys' clubs and YMCAs. If none of these facilities is available, the next best thing is to practice with a friend, or group of friends.

Forward Roll

This is the best stunt to start with. Stand erect at one end of
the mat, feet together, toes pointing forward.

Swing your arms up overhead and begin to lean forward into
the mat, bending your knees and shifting your weight to the balls
of your feet. When your hands touch the mat, kick off with your
toes and tuck your chin in toward your chest. Thus you will break
the roll with the back of your neck and shoulders, and will not
land on your head.

Now you "tuck"—roll your body into a tight ball. This is done
by bringing your thighs up to your chest and grasping your shins
as you continue rolling over and forward. Pull against your shins
to help bring your body forward and up to a standing position.

That's it—the important forward roll.

To make it a forward *dive*, practice pushing off from your toes
with greater momentum so that you actually get into the air,
landing on shoulder and back of neck and rolling forward in the
manner you've already learned. Take it easy. Don't try a running
dive right after you've learned the forward roll. Try an easy dive
from a standing position first, then move back a step or two and

(Above) Illus. 14: Kick off with your toes in the forward roll.

(Right) Illus. 15: Land on neck and shoulders in the forward roll.

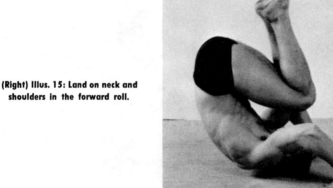

get a little more speed and height. *Then* you'll be ready to try a dive from a short run, and eventually from a long run. Work up to these things at your own rate. When you're learning, don't try to compete with your buddies. Everyone develops differently.

Learn the tuck well, and remember it. You'll encounter it again in the following stunts; it's a basic skill in tumbling, diving, acrobatics and trampolining.

Backward Roll

Stand erect, back to the mat. Sit backwards onto the mat, keeping your hands down at your sides, so as to break the fall with your hands and hips. Roll backward by pushing off with your legs, tucking your body into a tight roll. This will throw your legs over your head.

Swing your elbows up now and set your hands onto the mat slightly back of your neck. Continue rolling over in a tight tuck until your feet land on the mat, then push up with your hands and come to a full stand.

Illus. 16: The backward roll.

Learn the backward and forward rolls thoroughly. You should be able to do them easily and smoothly, controlling your speed and movement at every point. As you'll see later, in the section on self-defense, both the forward and backward rolls are essential in learning how to fall.

Headstand

Kneel on the mat, with your hands flat on the mat a shoulder-width apart. Bring your knees up to balance on your arms just above your elbows, legs parallel to the mat.

Tip your body forward until your head is resting on the mat. To get the proper spacing, your head and hands should be the three points of an equal-sided triangle on the mat. Push up slowly

(Below) Illus. 17: Beginning the headstand.

(Right) Illus. 18: The headstand completed.

with your hips and legs, balancing over the tripod formed by your head and hands. Arch your back to maintain balance.

It's helpful to have a friend or instructor hold your waist until you've learned the feel of headstand balance.

Handstand

Start off the same way as in the headstand, and push your hips and legs up and forward. Reach up with your legs, toes pointed, arching your back to achieve balance.

If you find this method too difficult, use the "kick-up." Kneel on the mat, then extend your legs out straight, so that only your toes and hands are touching the mat. Shift your balance forward so that all your weight is on your hands.

Illus. 19: Starting the handstand.

Then kick up with your legs, arching your back until you gain balance. If you still have trouble—*keep practicing*. You'll get it. The handstand isn't an easy stunt to master. It takes time to get the feel of proper balance.

Illus. 20: The handstand completed.

Forward Handspring

A handspring is a handstand in which you don't stand. Instead of balancing on your hands, your legs continue moving in an arc over your head and you land—hopefully—back on your feet.

After a short run toward the mat, throw your hands down to the mat at shoulder's width, arms straight and hands spread for wide support.

Kick one leg up first, then swing up with the other. As your legs

Illus. 21: Beginning the forward handspring.

Illus. 22: Near the peak of the forward handspring.

continue in an arc over your head, push off with your arms, arching your body high by pushing your hips upward. This will pull your shoulders up as your legs complete the arc and you land, feet together, on the mat.

(Above) Illus. 23: Past the peak of the forward handspring.

(Below) Illus. 24: Plan to land with feet together.

Arabian Handspring

That's just a fancy name for a handspring you take from a dive. Instead of coming down into a forward roll, you land on your hands and arch your legs over your head, as in the regular handspring. There's not a great deal of difference between the regular and the Arabian. It's a very handsome, impressive stunt, but requires extra practice.

The Back Bend

If you learn the back bend first, you'll find it easier to learn the back flip later. Stand with your back to the mat, feet about 12 inches apart. (Later, when you've developed good flexibility in your back and mastered the stunt, you'll be able to do the back bend with your feet closer together.)

Raise your arms up over your head and bend your knees. Slowly bend backward, maintaining your balance by keeping your hips balanced over your feet. You'll find you can do this by bending your knees more.

Illus. 26: The back bend.

Continue bending backward until you can reach the mat in back of you with your hands. Have a friend hold your waist at the

Illus. 27.

start. Once you have contact, distribute your weight equally over the four points of contact—both hands and feet.

There you are—gracefully arched in a back bend. *Now* what? How do you get out of it? It isn't considered cricket to just collapse onto the mat. Learning how to recover to your feet again isn't easy, but it's the only way to do it. It takes good strong muscles all over —in your thighs, abdomen, back and arms. One way to develop these muscles, of course, is to *practice* proper recovery. Another way is to strengthen your muscles with the kinds of exercises and weight training you'll find in the following chapters.

The first step is to try to push yourself up with your hands in order to balance your weight over your feet again. Bend your knees, thrust your hips forward and tighten your abdominal and thigh muscles to pull yourself up to a standing position. Swinging your arms up forward, toward your hips, will also help. But don't expect success on the first few tries.

The Front Flip

If you want to be formal, call it a forward somersault. Around the diving board or trampoline, though, most people simply call it a front flip. If you can do a forward roll from a dive, you can learn the front flip—eventually. Some people—a few—find it easy. Most people take their time in working up to it; it may take a few weeks, or as long as six months, depending on your own personality, physical ability, and the training available.

Take a short run up to the edge of the mat, then jump down (as for a dive) on both feet for the take-off. Aim for *height*, not distance. As you spring up, tuck your body into a tight ball: bring your chin down into your chest and pull your knees up to your chest, clasping your shins.

If you get off the ground with a good spring and go into a tight tuck, you shouldn't have any trouble performing a complete somersault. Keep your legs together as you turn, then open up from the tucked position in order to drop down to your feet.

Illus. 28: Going into the front flip.

Illus. 29: About to land in the front flip.

Bend your knees slightly to keep your balance and cushion the landing.

Illus. 30: Crouching for the
back flip.

The Back Flip

It takes a while to get from the forward roll to the forward
somersault, and it's an equal victory to proceed from the backward
roll to the back flip. Work up to it in gradual, progressive stages,
trying for a little more height each time.

From a standing position, crouch down on your toes in preparation for the upward throw. Swing your arms back, as you
would before a dive, and then throw them upward as you push
off straight up in the air with your legs. Throw your head back
immediately. This will automatically bring your shoulders and
arms up and back also. Bring your knees up into a tight tuck and
continue the circular roll backwards. Open up as you come around,
kicking out of the tuck with your legs. Bring your feet down and
swing your arms forward for the landing.

Illus. 31: On the way up in the back flip.

Illus. 32: Feet coming over in the back flip.

Illus. 33: Landing in the back flip.

The Cartwheel

If you've ever tried a cartwheel, you know it's not easy. Yet, like all athletic performances, it looks easy if it's done well. The cartwheel most youngsters do in school, by bending forward and tumbling around from hand to foot, is not really a cartwheel at all, of course.

There's only one solution: before you try a cartwheel, learn the handstand first. That's what a good cartwheel requires, as well as the ability to whip your body sideways into and out of a handstand. Instead of bending forward, in fact, you should be using the opposite kind of arch—the regular handstand arch.

Begin the cartwheel from a short skip to the side, whipping your body sideways and down, kicking up hard with the opposite leg. The other leg follows up as both hands support your body momentarily in a handstand. Your body spins through the handstand in a sideward arc as your feet swing over and down to the ground again.

Cartwheels are beautiful when they're well done; don't be discouraged if you find they take a long time to learn and perfect.

Continue practicing the handstand and the sideways whip, and you'll eventually master the stunt.

4. Setting-up Exercises

Many people make the mistake of starting a body-building program by lifting weights, without doing any preliminary exercises. Often they use weights that are too heavy, and then of course they become discouraged.

The first thing to remember is that you should never strain yourself with weights. You don't have to. But more about that later.

The second point is: Before you start any weight-lifting session, you should always do a series of setting-up exercises. You've probably had a taste of these calisthenics in school; they're also a regular part of the Basic Training programs in all of the Armed Forces.

It's easy—and wrong—to think that these exercises are unimportant because they're not done with weights. Setting-up exercises can keep you in good physical shape if you do them regularly—even if you never work with weights. They're not only designed to loosen, stretch, toughen, and warm up your muscles; they're also excellent body-builders in themselves. Give them half a chance and they'll keep you hard and trim.

You can do these exercises quickly, with snap and precision, after the first few sessions. In the beginning, don't work so fast that you run out of breath in a few minutes. Your motions should be smooth and rhythmic.

And don't forget to breathe. That may sound funny, but there's a natural tendency to hold your breath while exercising. You may not even be aware of it, so you should try to think about it consciously at first. Despite what you may have heard or read, there's no special way to breathe while exercising. Some people think you should breathe only through your nose. Others say, "Inhale through your nose, exhale through your mouth." And still others will tell you that athletes should breathe *only* through the mouth while exercising.

You can disregard all the special tricks. Not one of them has been "scientifically proven," as people will claim. The important thing is to breathe deeply, as often as you need, in a regular way. Breathe through your mouth whenever you need more air. Do whatever is most comfortable for you—but don't forget to breathe. It's an important part of the exercises.

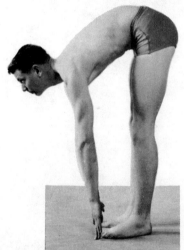

Illus. 35: Knees straight in the toe-toucher.

1. TOE-TOUCHER. Stand erect, hands on hips. *Keeping knees straight*, bend from waist and touch toes (or floor) with fingertips. Try 12 repetitions.

This is excellent for the abdominal muscles; the exercise is a well-known stomach-firmer and waist-reducer. As your suppleness increases, touch the floor with your palms, instead of your finger-tips.

2. SIDE-BENDER. Starting position: Stand erect, hands on hips. Bend forward at waist so that upper body is parallel to floor. Now proceed to rotate your upper body around in a loop, bending as far as you can in each direction. Do 12 repetitions—that is, 12 complete circles.

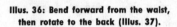

Illus. 36: Bend forward from the waist, then rotate to the back (Illus. 37).

Don't be afraid to stretch those muscles. Do the exercise in a smooth, swinging movement, without stopping or pausing. This doesn't make it easier, but harder, if you re doing the exercise right and really bending and stretching. This is an old military exercise, and still very effective. You can have strong arms and shoulders and legs, and still be weak if your trunk muscles are weak. The abdominal, back, and side muscles are the foundation of a solid, powerful body. Yet these are the weakest parts of the body in most men. That's why a number of these exercises are geared to strong abdominal and trunk development.

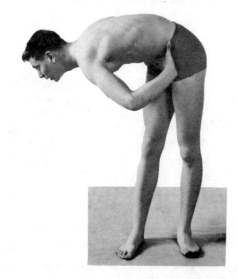

Illus. 38: The side rotation of the side-bender.

3. LEG-RAISER. In supine position (lying on back), place hands under hips, palms down on floor. Raise legs to vertical position,

Illus. 39: Keep feet together in the leg-raiser.

keeping feet together. Then lower them slowly, bringing heels to within a few inches of the floor, and hold legs in this position for four seconds. Try five repetitions for the first two weeks, then increase to 10.

You'll feel this in your abdominal muscles at first, but they'll soon toughen up. This is one of the finest exercises you can do. In just about a month it will give you a ripply, washerboard stomach, hard as a rock. The longer you can hold your legs off the floor, of course, the more you'll develop.

4. BICYCLE KICK. Lie on your back, hands at sides, palms down. Throw your legs into the air and move them in a rotating kick, as if riding a bicycle. Forming a supporting triangle, with hands on hips, elbows and arms on floor, is not good. It prevents your stomach and side muscles from getting most of the benefits of the exercise. Get your lower body up in the air as far as you can with your own trunk-power. Do 50 cycles with each leg.

After you have done this setting-up exercise for about two weeks,

Illus. 41: The bicycle kick.

regularly, your abdominal muscles will be strong enough to enable you to really kick out and kick hard. This kind of training can come in handy in a self-defense situation, since it's actually a basic jiu-jitsu technique. Just as certain wild animals fight very effectively from this position, using their feet and claws to attack and defend, and protect the stomach, so can you use it for strong kicking power if necessary. You can effectively stop the opponent who tries to jump you, and you can tangle his feet if thrown to the ground on your back.

5. SIT-UPS. Lie on back, hands at sides, feet together. Bring body to sitting position without bending knees or using hands or arms to push up. All the work is done by the abdominal and back muscles. Arms should rise slowly, roughly parallel to floor, as you sit up; do not stop when sitting position is reached, but

continue to bend forward and touch toes with fingertips. Try 12 repetitions.

6. PUSH-UPS. Start in prone position (lying on stomach). Place hands on floor, a shoulder's-width apart. Keeping back straight, push yourself up to arm's length, then lower yourself until chest or chin touches floor; then push up again. Begin with 10 repetitions, and continue to increase the number until you can do 25 or 30 push-ups in good form.

It is important to keep the body straight, for proper form: no sagging in the middle, no hunching up. All the work is done with the arms and shoulders. This is especially good for the triceps and deltoids. (See pages 57 and 58 for Muscle Chart.)

Illus. 43: The push-up, starting position.

Illus. 44: Good form in a push-up.

5. Should You Lift Weights?

In the second chapter, we mentioned the "six-second theory" of muscle growth. The theory may be a good one. Until it is better established and more widely accepted in this country, however, we'll have to rely on weight-lifting as the best, fastest, and most successful method of muscle-building yet discovered. It is a proven method, and the best way to prove it for yourself is to try it. Anybody who lifts weights progressively and regularly every other day for just three or four months will see tremendous gains in muscular growth and strength.

Today, weight-training is used by a great many athletes. Not only boxers and wrestlers, but also basketball, baseball and football players, and even track men, swimmers and judo experts, know they can improve their performance by training with weights. *All* athletes can.

Bob Kiphuth, the famous Yale swimming coach, knew the secret, too. Are you familiar with the incredible statistics? Over a 41-year period, the crack Yale team swam in 508 meets—and lost only four. Kiphuth trained his men on dry land for two solid months at the beginning of each season. They didn't swim. The only time they got under water was in the shower room. What kind of training did they get? Weight-training, and exercises: a routine muscle-building course.

We'll get into weight-lifting exercises in the next chapter. First, let's clear the air. There are a lot of people who still believe the old superstition that lightning never strikes twice in the same place, and there are also a lot of people who still believe the old superstitions about weight-lifting.

Are weight-lifters sluggish, muscular dolts who can barely bend their arms? Can weight-lifting make you musclebound? Is it "unnatural"? Will it hinder your flexibility? Today we know that all these questions can be answered simply: No.

As for flexibility, remember this: judo is a sport that requires a great deal of flexibility, and *judo champions train with weights.* So do gymnasts and acrobats, the most graceful and flexible of athletes.

You will not lose any flexibility or speed by developing your muscles. On the contrary, you'll gain in both areas. When coaches and athletes realized this, they began to use weight-training to great advantage. Today almost everybody uses it.

So don't let anybody kid you about the so-called dangers of weight-training. The ones who talk about getting musclebound are either envious or misinformed. There's no longer any question about it. Sports College, the independent research organization, says that training with weights can increase your proficiency in *any* sport, and that fears of becoming musclebound are unnecessary.

The athlete who uses weights is faster, stronger, lighter on his feet, and far more graceful and flexible than the average athlete who doesn't use weights. His endurance is better, and his heart and lungs and internal organs are stronger and healthier.

So much for superstitions. Now the question is: how do your muscles grow?

Muscles are made up of tiny muscle fibres—about four billion of them in your body. The average muscle fibre is about $1\frac{1}{4}$ inches in length, and 1/600 of an inch in diameter. If all your muscle fibres could be stretched out into one long thread, it could circle the globe four times!

What does exercise do to these fibres? It doesn't increase the *number* of fibres, but rather the size of the individual fibres. As you exercise, the parts of the fibre that have never worked before begin to work. Connective tissue becomes thicker and tougher. The tiny blood capillaries that feed the fibres increase in number. It's important that you know this, because these little capillaries are an essential factor in muscle growth. They bring oxygen and glycogen to the muscle fibres, and they carry waste material— mostly lactic acid—away from the fibres. You should lift weights every other day, rather than every day; the resting days provide time for the capillaries to grow. If you didn't give them time, you'd get a heavy accumulation of lactic acid in your body, and this brings on fatigue. So take the cue from your body, and give yourself plenty of rest.

Should you lift weights? By all means. Remember to do some warm-up exercises first, and also remember that weight-lifting is probably the most strenuous form of exercise known. I am assuming, of course, that there is nothing seriously wrong with your health to begin with. If you have had any kind of heart trouble, you should not attempt to lift weights unless you have first received permission from your doctor. There are many handicapped people who can benefit greatly from supervised weight-training.

Make sure you're in good health. Get a physical checkup before you begin, and tell your doctor you plan to start a weight-lifting program. When you have his consent—go to it!

6. Weight-Lifting

To most body-builders, weight-lifting is a very stimulating and enjoyable activity. To others, it is simply hard work—but well worth it. One thing is certain: there are no short-cuts. Once you decide to build your body by lifting weights, you must stick to it if you expect to see results. It isn't a system that works for some, and not for others. If you do stick to it, you *will* get results—and very satisfying ones. Weight-lifting will work for anyone who stays with it for just a few months.

Here are some terms you should know:

A *repetition* is one complete motion of a single exercise.

A specified number of repetitions—12, for instance, in the bench press—makes up a single *set*.

Definition refers to the sharpness of the muscle outline.

How to Exercise

Your weight-lifting session should never become a furious, breathtaking activity. It is important to rest between sets. If you are of average build, rest from three to five minutes between sets.

If you are underweight and want to gain, do fewer repetitions with slightly heavier weights, and take four- to five-minute rests between sets.

If you are overweight, or have considerable muscle bulk and

want greater definition, do more repetitions with somewhat lighter weights, and take shorter rests between sets. One to two minutes is sufficient.

Breathe regularly while exercising, as often and as deeply as you need. Never try to hold your breath. It is especially good to breathe deeply when doing the bench press.

It is not necessary to put an extra strain or tension on your muscles when exercising. The act of lifting the weight for the proper number of repetitions, and in correct form, will automatically tense the proper muscles.

When to Exercise

The amount of time you spend, and the regularity of your training, are both very important factors.

Don't make the mistake of trying to plunge in by lifting every day. No weight-lifter does. You should have three or four training periods a week, on alternate days. Each period should last from one to two hours. (Not all of this time should be devoted to weight-lifting activity. You should spend about twenty minutes or a half-hour in warming up with the exercises described in Chapter 4.)

Thus, you will be lifting weights one day, and resting the next. The resting days are just as important as the training days. Your muscles will grow, and your body will rest and rebuild itself, on the days off.

People who keep in shape with light calisthenics, or setting-up exercises, often like to do them in the morning, as soon as they awaken. The best time for weight-lifting, however, is at the other end of the day—in the evening, preferably just before going to bed. The reason for this will be clear after your first few sessions: weight-lifting is hard work. You will want to rest after lifting, and you won't want to tire yourself out at the beginning of the day.

As with swimming, you should wait at least a half hour after eating before exercising. If you are lifting weights in the late afternoon, plan your training session so that it ends about a half hour before your evening meal.

Food and Weight Control

One of the most attractive features of weight-lifting is that it tends to balance out your body. If you are overweight, it will help you reduce, and replace excess fat with muscle. If you are thin and underweight, it will build you up.

Nevertheless, all body-builders agree that diet is still the most important factor in controlling body weight. If you are underweight, your diet should include plenty of good, wholesome food: meat, butter, eggs, fresh fruits and vegetables, and plenty of milk and water every day. You can afford to eat the richer, fattier foods to help you put on a little weight: spaghetti and meatballs, mashed potatoes, and so on. But avoid heavily-seasoned foods.

And of course you should get plenty of rest. If you are under 21, you should be getting at least eight hours of sleep, and nine or ten is better.

If you are overweight, there is no substitute for cutting down on the *amount* of food you eat. Make sure that your diet is wholesome, rather than sweet or starchy. Keep away from fatty foods; eat baked potatoes without butter instead of mashed, and try to add more fish, chicken, calves' liver, and fresh fruits and vegetables to your meals.

The Basic Six

There are hundreds of different kinds of exercises you can do with weights, but most of them are far too specialized for the beginner. When you're starting out, you should concentrate on the exercises contained in these two chapters on weight-lifting. This chapter includes what many experts consider the Basic Six exercises: the bench press, regular press, squats, rowing motion, curls, and dead lift.

A great many of the specialized exercises are simply variations of these, designed to build up smaller muscle-groups for better definition.

As we take a closer look at the Basic Six, you'll see that each of them is an important exercise with a definite job to do. If you were to do nothing more than these six exercises, every other day for three months, you'd be astounded at your muscular improvement.

That doesn't mean, of course, that you *should* do "nothing more than these six exercises" for the next three months. A number of other important exercises are described in the following chapter, and the best program is to do half the total exercises on alternate training days.

For example, let's say that you've decided to exercise on Mondays, Wednesdays, and Fridays, and rest on Tuesdays, Thursdays, and weekends. On the first Monday, you would do two sets of the Basic Six. That means that you would go through the six exercises with the proper number of repetitions for each one, and then start at the beginning and go through the cycle of six exercises again.

On Tuesday you rest. On Wednesday you would do two sets of the exercises in the next chapter, and on the following Monday you would be back on the Basic Six.

Some people prefer to exercise every other day, including weekends, rather than three days a week, especially when they are starting out. This is perfectly all right; three days of rest per week is sufficient. But of course they should be *alternate* days. It would be very poor training to work out for four straight days, and rest for three.

The important thing is to choose a training schedule that you find convenient, and stick to it. *Regular* training with weights is the real "secret" of successful body-building. Occasional bursts of heavy training will do little if any good, and may be positively harmful.

In explaining the exercises, I have generally used the anatomical names for all muscles. You can learn them quickly by referring to the illustrated charts of body muscles in this chapter. Since these terms are actually used by body-builders and weight-lifters, and by many coaches and athletes, you will want to become familiar with them.

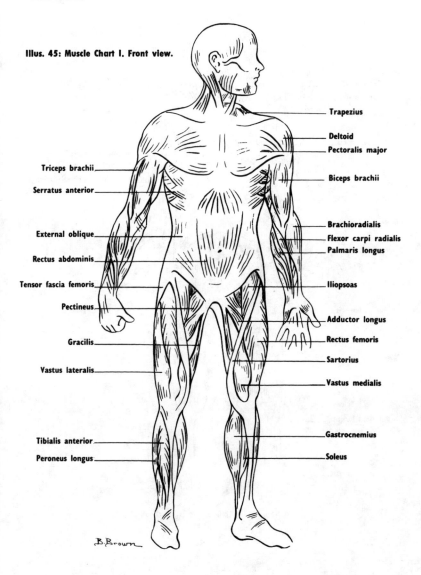

Illus. 45: Muscle Chart I. Front view.

Trapezius

Deltoid
Pectoralis major

Triceps brachii

Biceps brachii

Serratus anterior

Brachioradialis
Flexor carpi radialis
Palmaris longus

External oblique

Rectus abdominis

Tensor fascia femoris

Iliopsoas

Pectineus

Adductor longus

Gracilis

Rectus femoris

Sartorius

Vastus lateralis

Vastus medialis

Tibialis anterior

Gastrocnemius

Peroneus longus

Soleus

B. Brown

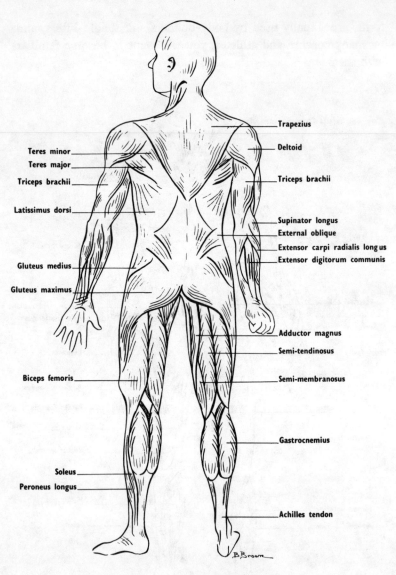

Teres minor

Teres major

Triceps brachii

Latissimus dorsi

Gluteus medius

Gluteus maximus

Biceps femoris

Soleus

Peroneus longus

Trapezius

Deltoid

Triceps brachii

Supinator longus

External oblique

Extensor carpi radialis longus

Extensor digitorum communis

Adductor magnus

Semi-tendinosus

Semi-membranosus

Gastrocnemius

Achilles tendon

B. Brown

Illus. 46: Muscle Chart II. Back view.

1. The *bench press* is the best single exercise for fast chest development. Specifically, it builds up the pectoral muscles, frontal deltoids, and triceps.

2. The *regular press* develops the arms (triceps) and shoulders.

3. *Squats* are the best-known leg developers—a popular exercise in paratrooper training units. Squats are excellent for building up the thighs, lungs and rib cage.

4. The *rowing motion* builds a strong back by developing the latissimus dorsi muscles, trapezius, and rear deltoids.

5. *Curls* are the famous biceps-builders, essential for strong arms.

6. The rowing motion develops the upper and middle parts of the back and sides; *dead lifts* take care of the all-important lower back muscle, or spinal erector.

How to Do the Basic Six

1. BENCH PRESS. Sometimes also called the back press, this requires the use of a low, sturdy bench and two bar supports. The bar supports are used to support the barbells while you take up your position on the bench. (If you're working with a partner, the bar supports are not absolutely necessary. He can hand the barbell to you when you're comfortably situated on the bench.)

Adjust the equipment so that you can first sit on the end of the bench with your knees bent comfortably, feet touching the floor. Then lie back on the bench so that your shoulders are under the barbell. Now you are in position to bring your hands back to your shoulders and grasp the barbell.

(Work with a light weight for the first two weeks: 30 or 40 pounds will be sufficient. Gradually work up to 50 pounds by adding 10 pounds per week; thereafter, continue to increase the weight slowly as you develop.)

Remove the barbell from the bar supports, or take it from your partner. Starting from chest level, push the barbell up to arms'

(Above) Illus. 47: The bench press. Your partner hands you the barbell if you do not have bar supports. (Below) Illus. 48: He stands by while you do the exercise.

Illus. 49: The bench press completed.

length, and return to chest level. Breathe deeply as you push upwards. Do 12 repetitions.

2. REGULAR PRESS. One of the three official Olympic lifts, this is also called the Two-Hands Military Press. In this press,

Illus. 50.

the weight is lifted with both hands straight from the floor to shoulder level in one continuous movement; then, after a two-second pause, the weight is pushed straight up to arms' length overhead. It is this latter movement that is properly called a press.

(Above) Illus. 51: The regular press, starting position.

(Below) Illus. 52: Press to arms length.

The regular press is executed by pushing the barbell up from shoulder level, and returning it to shoulder level. The movement should be smooth and clean. Try to avoid jerky, uneven motions.

All the work is done by the arms and shoulders. The head and body are kept in a vertical position, and the legs are straight and stationary. It is important to avoid the natural tendency to arch the back. Do 12 repetitions, using a 30- or 40-pound weight.

3. SQUATS. In calisthenics, these are called Deep Knee Bends. In weight-lifting, and in the various Armed Forces, they're usually known as squats. A wonderful exercise, squats will develop powerful legs, and an enormous chest and lung capacity.

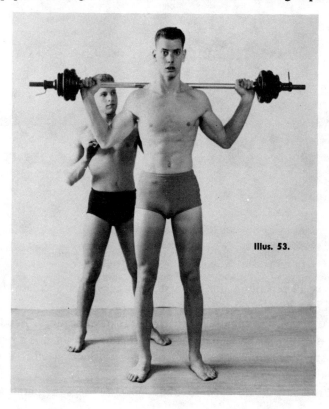

Illus. 53.

But quantity is as important here as quality: you must work up to a good number of repetitions, and they must be done right.

Place the bar of the barbell against the back of your neck and squat down, making sure to keep your head up and your back perfectly straight; then return to standing position. Use 40 or 50 pounds of weight.

Illus. 54: The squat with barbell. Work with a partner.

Try 12 repetitions for the first two weeks, then increase slowly to 15 or 20.

After the first month, when your legs have begun to build up, do as many *free squats* daily as you can. The free squat is a regular calisthenic, performed without using any weight at all, but with hands placed on hips.

Free squats are used to build powerful legs in paratrooper

(Left) Illus. 55: The squat from side view.

(Below) Illus. 56: Completed.

training units. Even in Army basic training, a soldier must be able to do 75 free squats in order to achieve a grade of 100% in this exercise during the physical training tests. This is not to say, unfortunately, that every soldier can do it; but every body-builder should eventually work up to 100 squats.

A former body-builder in California recently decided to become a professional wrestler, and was dissatisfied with the size and strength of his legs. He put himself on a rigorous schedule of squats (free-style), and finally worked up to 1000 a day, in sets of 200 each. His chest and lungs benefited tremendously, of course, as well as his thighs, which finally measured 26 inches around. It can be done; but remember that he was a body-builder in fine shape to begin with.

(Left) Illus. 57: The free squat.

(Below) Illus. 58: Completed.

When you first begin, you'll find your thighs beginning to feel it after 20 or 25 free squats. Of course you should never push yourself to the point of exhaustion; take it easy in the beginning. After the first week or two, you won't have to worry about "straining" your thighs. They're the biggest, strongest muscles in your body, and they can take it.

4. ROWING MOTION. If you're looking for that V-shaped upper body, this is the exercise for you. The rowing motion develops not only the rear deltoids and the strong *trapezius* muscle in the center of the upper back, but also the *latissimus dorsi* or "wing" muscles—the ones that flare up from the sides of the rib cage right to the shoulders.

Illus. 59.

Illus. 60.

Bend at the waist so that upper body is parallel to the ground. Keep your legs and back straight. Pull the weight straight up to the neck, using your arms and shoulders to do all the work. Elbows are kept out wide, away from the body. Then lower barbell to straight-arm position. Do 12 repetitions, using 30 or 40 pounds to start.

5. CURLS. Whatever else you may be looking for, it's a sure bet you're in the market for a strong and powerful pair of arms. The biceps are the universal symbol of masculine strength. Trainees in most of the Armed Forces are required to do eight or ten pull-ups on the chinning bar before every meal. Yet, when they start basic training, many men can't get beyond the first two or three—and some can't chin themselves once. A great many boys neglect their arms because they seldom have to use them in civilian life. It's

Illus. 61: The curl with barbell.

a vicious circle: the boy who feels that his arms are weak may be afraid to play baseball and football—the very sports that could develop his arms.

You need solid arm power for throwing, lifting, pushing, pulling, climbing, hanging, carrying—and, in an emergency, for self-defense fighting. The weight-lifter's curl is the best and fastest way to develop the all-important biceps muscle.

A regular overhand grip was used in all the previous exercises. In the normal curl, an underhand grip is used to develop the biceps. An overhand grip is used (reverse curl) to build up the forearm muscles as well as the biceps.

Either a barbell or dumbbells may be used. Start with 15 or

Illus. 62: The curl, regular underhand grip.

20 pounds, and work up to 30 or more. Stand erect, holding weight at arms' length. Bring the weight in a semi-circular path up to shoulder level, keeping elbows at sides. The back is kept straight; don't allow yourself to bend backwards or move your elbows back. Do 12 repetitions.

Illus. 63: The curl, reverse (overhand) grip.

6. DEAD-LIFT. Two grips are possible: a regular overhand grip, or a combination grip—one hand over, one under. Use whichever you prefer. Some body-builders like to use the combination grip when the barbell is straddled.

In the starting position, the weight is on the floor. It may either be straddled, or approached from one side. Grasp the bar, keeping arms straight, and simply straighten the legs and body. Lifting is done with the lower back muscles, not with the arms or shoulders. Do 10 repetitions.

In the beginning, use a light weight—not more than 60 pounds. Slowly work up to 75 and 100.

A note of caution here: No matter how powerful your arms and shoulders may be, never try to lift a heavy weight from the ground unless you've been doing dead-lifts in your weight-training program. The lower back muscle, or spinal erector, is an important

(Above) Illus. 64: The dead lift, straddle position.

(Below) Illus. 65: Note the combination grip.

Illus. 66: The dead lift, approach from the side.

foundation muscle, enabling you to walk upright. With regular attention and development, it will become a powerful muscle, capable of supporting tremendous amounts of weight. It can be strained, however, if you attempt a heavy dead-lift without previous training.

Therefore, start your program with a weight you can handle easily, and you'll never have any trouble. The rule for safety is this: In the dead-lift, never use a weight that you cannot lift without straining for at least five repetitions.

Illus. 67: The dead lift, regular overhand grip.

7. Interesting Exercises

The Basic Six exercises are designed to build the major muscle groups—arms, back, chest, trunk and thighs. But you can also use your imagination to make up your own exercises. Almost any exercise you do, no matter how unusual, is good, as long as you don't overdo it. Here are six to start with—specialized exercises to build your calf muscles, which are likely to be ignored, and other muscle groups you'll want to develop. After you've worked on these, think up your own variations if you find your training program getting monotonous.

Calf-Builder

A fairly common mistake of beginners is to concentrate on building just the upper body. Even if you include squats, poor calf development can spoil the effect of an otherwise excellent physique. Here's how to look good from the knees down.

Standing erect, feet apart, support the barbell across the shoulders against the back of your neck. With your hands grasp the bar near the inside collars.

Keeping your back and legs straight, slowly raise up as high as possible on your toes; then return to standing position.

Start with 24 repetitions. You'll get the best results if you do

12 times with your toes pointed out and the next 12 with toes pointed in. This is the surest way to develop both parts of the two-headed calf muscle, or *gastrocnemius*.

Illus. 68: The calf-builder.

Some body-builders stand with the balls of their feet on a plank or 2×4, so that heels can be lowered down to the floor, thus stretching and building calf muscles even more. This is not essential, and some physical education specialists do not recommend it, while others do. In any case, you shouldn't worry about it until you're ready for advanced development; then it's up to you.

Start with a 30- or 40-pound barbell for this exercise and work up to about half your body weight. If you weigh less than 100 pounds, start with a 20-pound weight and work up.

Pull-Over

This is good for developing the flaring *latissimus dorsi* muscles of the back, and the *pectoralis major* (chest muscles).

Lie on your back with your knees drawn up to your chest, legs crossed at the ankles, feet not touching the floor. Extend your arms beyond the head, elbows locked so that arms are straight. Use light dumbbells, 10 pounds each, or just the bar of a barbell with no weights added.

Illus. 69: The pull-over. You may prefer to keep both legs on the mat.

To do one repetition, raise the weight in a short 90-degree arc to a position directly above the chest, keeping arms and back straight; then return to starting position. It is important to do the work with your chest and side muscles, and without arching your back. Do 10 repetitions.

Press Behind Neck

This is like the regular press, except that you start with the barbell resting on your shoulders against the back of your neck—

Illus. 70: The press behind the neck.

the same starting position used for the calf-builder. Press the bar up to arms' length overhead, then lower it to starting position. Keep the knees and back straight.

Illus. 71: Completed.

This press, in addition to building the triceps and shoulders, will also develop the important *trapezius* muscle of the upper back; and it's an excellent exercise if you're round-shouldered. So is the pull-over, above. Do 12 repetitions.

Side-Bend

Muscles often ignored or neglected by beginners are those at the sides of the waist, called the external and internal oblique muscles. They shouldn't be forgotten; side-bending is important in developing a strong trunk.

You can do the exercise with a dumbbell or barbell. Since both methods are good, you can use them in alternate training sessions.

Illus. 72: The side-bend.

1. Place the bar across your shoulders, behind your neck, as in the preceding exercise. Use just the bar; side-bends should be done with the same amount of weight you use in the curl. Bend to one side as far as possible, then to the other side, and return to the starting position. That's one repetition. Don't bend your knees or allow yourself to bend forward. All the work should be done at the waist. Start with 10 repetitions and slowly work up to 20, adding weight when you feel you can use it.

2. Use a single dumbbell. Stand erect, arms at sides, holding the dumbbell in your right hand. Bend to the right side, then to the left, and back to the starting position. Again, that counts as one repetition. Do 10 times with the dumbbell in your right hand, then 10 with the weight in your left.

Shoulder Shrug

This is a specialized exercise to develop the diamond-shaped *trapezius* muscle, which slopes down from the back of the neck out to the deltoids, and then down to converge at the center of the back.

Illus. 73: The shoulder shrug.

Stand erect, feet apart, holding the barbell at arms' length across your thighs. Grasp the bar near the inside collars.

The action is simple. Lift your shoulders upward as far as possible in a slow shrug, keeping the arms straight.

Start with a 30- or 40-pound barbell and gradually work up to about half your body weight. At first, do 12 repetitions.

Alternate Press

Extra work on curls can produce good biceps, but it's the triceps that give your upper arms a full, rounded effect and add a great deal of strength. This alternate press, done with dumbbells, develops the triceps and deltoids.

Stand erect, feet apart, holding dumbbells at shoulder level. (Use a weight you can handle, between 10 and 25 pounds. Add weight later, as you develop.)

Illus. 74: The alternate press.

Lift the weight in your right hand to arm's length overhead, then lower to shoulder level. As the right arm is lowered, push the dumbbell in the left hand up to arm's length. Continue this alternate movement for 10 repetitions. One repetition is completed when you have done a press with both arms.

When you want variety or special emphasis on a particular muscle group, you can find many other exercises in books and magazines devoted to weight training. And remember: There's nothing wrong with making up your own variations.

8. Self-Defense

The rest of this book deals with self-defense. You should understand that there are a number of self-defense techniques, all of them very effective. Many people in this country have heard about *karate* by now, but there are still plenty who think that all methods of unarmed defense are called *judo*. Judo is a highly specialized sport, with a definite etiquette, forms and throws. Kicking, for example, is not a part of judo; striking out with the hands is not judo. Judo today is practiced as a sport, although it was developed as a method of self-defense.

In addition to judo and karate, there is *savate*, the French method of foot-defense; *jiu-jitsu*, includes judo but has additional throws, chops, and special defenses; *aikido* is the art of twisting and bending the joints, and taking advantage of your opponent's maneuvers; *yawara* is used in conjunction with aikido to provide effective wrist-holds, arm-locks, body-holds, and chokes, and the defenses against all of these.

The list is far from exhausted. There is the excellent and scientific Chinese method of *cheena-adi*, a kind of judo-jiu-jitsu combination; the Indian art of *lathie*, or stick defense; the Japanese *kempo*, a "hard" art of self-defense against armed opponents; and even the Irish *shillelagh*, or cudgel-play. There is

American Marine fighting, a combination of jiu-jitsu, boxing, wrestling, brawling, and a few other techniques thrown in. The Indian *Gusthi*, or wrestling, is also a form of sporting combat.

So remember that judo is but a single art, an excellent one, but hardly the last word on self-defense. The methods described in the following chapters are actually called *ketsugo*—the Japanese word for combination. These methods represent the best and most basic techniques, selected from a number of the different forms of self-defense mentioned above. Only the throws can really be called judo.

What about the men who have mastered these skills—what are they like? It's interesting that they have a characteristic philosophy and disposition. They're almost always of a gentle, pleasant, and peaceable nature. Why? Well—why not? They can afford to be. They wouldn't think of starting or provoking a fight, because they have no need to prove themselves. They've demonstrated their powers many times. Instead of chips on their shoulders, they have quiet, firm confidence in their own abilities.

They learn these techniques, not in order to be aggressive fighters or troublemakers, but simply to be able to protect and defend themselves and their families.

Most of these methods, in fact, were developed hundreds of years ago in Asia and the Orient, often by peasants and monks who had no weapons. This was the only way they could defend themselves against the numerous bandits and robbers who roamed the countryside at night.

Throughout the world, those who have learned these methods have always retained the ancient philosophy of self-defense: Never provoke or encourage a fight. Fight only to protect and defend yourself, or someone who is being bullied. Maintain a high regard for gentlemanly conduct and good sportsmanship. Some of the world's top-ranking judo experts have been praised by their fellows for refusing to demonstrate their powers when provoked by mere words. They will defend themselves, of course, if attacked, but they will never "demonstrate" just to show off. (Official judo demonstrations, tournaments, and exhibitions are not in the "show-off" category.)

I have never met or heard of a self-defense expert who was not a person of honor and courtesy.

As you increase your skill in self-defense, you'll find that you're automatically better at keeping your wits about you in a dangerous situation. You won't scare as easily. This is one of the wonderful benefits of self-defense training.

A few years ago, a small group of people were sitting in a café in New York City. There were two young ladies in the group, and one of them happened to be unusually pretty. There was also a judo expert in the party—a mild, pleasant man in his fifties.

These people were annoyed by a group of wise-talking hoodlums who made remarks about the girl. One of them finally came up and put his hand on her shoulder. He had no sooner touched her than he was thrown back violently against the wall by the old judo expert—*who never left his chair!*

The rest of the gang came at him, and went flying. The judo expert remained seated; he was merely moving his arms, with apparently little effort. In fact, he continued talking to the group all this time!

Yes, it sounds incredible. But it's quite true. The man, of course, was a judo master, with a lifetime of practice and training behind him. There wasn't much he didn't know about balance and self-defense. And any judo expert will tell you that it's quite possible to throw somebody while you're sitting in a chair, if you know your judo.

How Important Is Strength?

Judo is often referred to as "the *gentle* art of self-defense." While it is true that no great strength is needed to master most of these self-defense techniques, it would be foolish to think that strength is not important. In man-to-man combat, strength is always important. It may not be the decisive factor, but only an expert in self-defense can afford to disregard it.

If we were to set up a contest between two students who had identical skill in judo, but were of unequal strength, the stronger would win every time. It's a mistake to think that you can rely solely on self-defense tricks and fast maneuvers. Speed and clever strategy are good; indeed, they are essential. But they may not be enough. They can be used to best advantage only when the body is strong and flexible. While regular self-defense training will itself help to toughen the body, it should be supplemented by a vigorous program of body-building and weight-training. This is the kind of program used by the world judo champions.

How to Practice

Every self-defense technique involves a certain logical sequence of steps. They must be described that way, and you will find it easiest to practice that way—first you do this, then that, and now this. What you should aim for, though, is not a series of individual movements, but one smooth, speedy, continuous motion.

When you practice with a partner, go through the motions slowly, even stopping if necessary to refer to the pictures and text again. Make sure your balance, body position, and stance are right at each point. Continue in this manner, slow-motion, until you are able to blend the movements together slowly. Then increase your speed. Repeat the entire technique a few times to make sure you have learned it; now let your partner practice.

These techniques have been described from the point of view of the right-handed person. Once you have gained proficiency from this side, of course, you should reverse the directions and practice them from the left side as well. No matter how long you train in judo, you can't begin to call yourself an expert until you can perform any maneuver from either side.

What to Wear

Assuming that you do not have a regular judo outfit, remember to wear old and sturdy clothes when practicing. Dungarees are

Illus. 76: The judo costume.

excellent. The shirt is sometimes a problem: ideally, it should be heavy enough to resist being torn. Otherwise, it should be old enough so that it won't matter if it is torn. A sturdy work-shirt will usually do the trick.

Where to Practice

The use of a mat is recommended wherever possible. However, lack of a mat should not prevent you from practicing most of these self-defense techniques. A soft, grassy area, free of stones and other debris, will serve just as well. Putting down a couple of blankets is good, too. The shoulder and somersault throws are the only ones that require a padded mat.

Balance

In all self-defense, balance is the essential element. The object, of course, is to maintain your own balance while breaking or disturbing your opponent's.

Your balance will be "weak to the front"—meaning you have poor balance, and can be pulled or pushed forward easily—when your weight is on the toes of both feet. It is "weak to the back" when your weight is on both heels; you can be pushed or pulled backwards easily.

The weakest position of all is that in which you balance on one foot. Here you may be pushed easily in any direction.

In the *strongest* fighting position, the feet are perpendicular (at right angles) to one another, and the body is twisted slightly, as in Illustration 77.

Practice your balance. Again I emphasize that this is the most important part of self-defense. Some beginners fail to realize this, because they have come to judo after hearing "you don't have to be strong."

It is the gentle art—but why? Why is it called the *soft* art, the *yielding* art? Because that's just what you do. You yield— up to a point. You act weak, as though you're a pushover.

Let's say an antagonist is pushing you around. He puts his big fat paws on your chest and pushes. What do *you* do?

You let him push. Try to stand firm, as though you're simply resisting him; but don't step forward, and don't push back.

Illus. 77: The fighting stance. A strong balance position.

When he feels resistance, the bully pushes harder. Now you might take half a step back, or two or three small steps if he's really much stronger.

Who has the advantage of balance at this point? You do, of course. You're standing still, or taking very short steps backward. You can easily maintain your center of balance.

But your opponent is pushing forward, and leaning forward.

So instead of pushing back, you quickly grab his wrists or coat-sleeves, and *pull him forward*—hard. Chances are Bully Doakes will fall flat on his face, as he pitches past you.

That, very simply, is what we mean when we talk about taking advantage of your opponent's balance. All judo throws, and many other self-defense techniques, are designed to catch the other guy off balance, or *put* him off balance, and give you the upper hand.

The Starting Position

When working on the throws with a partner, always assume the standard judo starting position. Facing partner, grasp the underside of his right sleeve, just below the elbow, with your left hand, and his left lapel with your right hand. Your partner takes the same grip on you.

Illus. 78: The starting position and grip.

In a self-defense situation, you would try to grip your opponent in roughly the same way, whenever possible.

How to Move

Once you have the grip, you and your partner begin to move and maneuver about the mat. The way you move is important. Don't pick your feet up too high; you're more likely to lose your balance that way. The best technique is a kind of gliding movement, in which the feet slide lightly over the mat, sometimes touching it, and seldom lifted more than an inch. Try not to cross one foot in front or in back of the other—that also weakens your balance.

9. How to Fall

If you don't want to get hurt, learn how to fall. If you want to build up your confidence for self-defense training, learn how to fall. If you ever expect to go on to advanced judo, learn how to fall.

In short, you *must* learn how to fall. This is the most important part of your preparation. Don't make the mistake that most beginners do: They ignore the falls because the falls don't seem important or because they think they already know how to fall.

If you were to sit in on any judo class, you'd see that the students spend the first lesson or two just on falls. After that, they devote at least ten minutes of each session practicing and warming up on falls; and this includes the most advanced students and judo masters.

Why is it so important? Simply because you can't practice this kind of self-defense unless you do know how to fall. It's too dangerous. You can get hurt badly without a good falling technique; but *with* a good technique, there's little or no chance that you'll hurt yourself at all.

Where will you be when you really need your self-defense training? You won't be on a mat. You may not be on grass. You may very well be in the city, or on a hard concrete or asphalt surface, and possibly walking along with a date.

If you get knocked down, knowing how to fall will keep you

from getting hurt, and it will help you to bounce back up. Once you learn how to fall, hard surfaces won't be as dangerous. After a month or two of practice, you'll automatically fall the right way. There's nothing magical about falling; you can still get scratched or bruised on a hard surface, but that's a lot better than breaking a bone or hitting your head. The best way to warm up for any self-defense practice is to work on your falls.

The most important thing is to roll with the fall, which means that your body goes into a natural curl as soon as you start to fall. It does not mean that you just crumple up, or relax like a soggy dishrag. In the curl, your chin is tucked down onto your chest, and your knees are pulled up toward your chest.

Illus. 79: The natural falling curl.

Never try to break your fall with stiff arms, or with your hands out. Your aim in falling is to develop an easy, controlled roll. The body should not be tense; you can maintain the curl without being stiff.

While you don't break your fall with stiff arms or hands out, you do use your arms to break the fall, in this way: just as you hit the mat or ground, slap down hard with your arm. (Whether you

Illus. 80: Breaking the fall.

use both arms or just one will depend on the kind of fall you're taking.)

Using your arm (or arms) to break the fall this way accomplishes three things: it gives you a natural shock-absorber, helps you bring the roll to a stop, and prepares you for a quick recovery and rebound to your feet.

To understand the arm motion clearly, lie on your back on the mat, with your head forward and chin tucked into your chest and your knees drawn up toward your head. Keep your arms extended flat, palms down, for support. This is the actual position in which you land in the backward fall. Now raise your arms up well in the air, and bring them down hard on the mat, letting them bounce up naturally. This is what actually breaks your fall.

Your whole arm, from shoulder to fingertips, should strike the mat at the same time. If you keep your arms relaxed during this motion, you'll find that you won't get hurt. But this does not mean that you should hit the mat lightly. On the contrary, don't be afraid to hit it hard. "Relaxed" means that your arms should not be stiff, and the muscles should not be tense.

Your arms should always be in front of you when you're falling, and should hit the mat first.

Let's consider the four basic falls in more detail. Practice them in order, since they range from the easiest and most common (falls to the side) to the most unusual and difficult (forward fall from stand). The falls to the side and back are by far the most useful, and should be mastered thoroughly before you go on to the others.

Falls to the Side

ROLLS TO RIGHT AND LEFT. Assume the same position as before, lying on your back with your body curled, head forward (chin tucked in), and knees drawn up toward chest. Instead of bringing

Illus. 81: The rolling fall to the right.

Illus. 82: The middle of the alternate roll.

both arms up, however, this time roll to your right, and strike the mat with your right arm to break the "fall." Your left arm should be folded across your chest in a comfortable position.

Practice the same roll to the left, beating the mat with your left arm.

ALTERNATE ROLL TO BOTH SIDES. Now combine the two, so that you're rolling in a continuous movement from one side to the other, striking the mat with the proper arm each time. This is an excellent warm-up, since it will introduce you to the roll and help you get acquainted with the feeling of movement in a good curl position.

There is no special number of "times" to do this exercise; there is a natural tendency, as in weight-lifting, to concentrate on the count rather than on the proper form. It's easy to cheat yourself without meaning to. Therefore, do the alternate roll until you've had enough, but always concentrate on doing it *well*, which really means three things:

1. Keep your head forward always, chin tucked in.

Illus. 83: The rolling fall to the left.

2. Beat down hard with the proper arm. In the backward fall, use both arms.

3. Keep your arms and body-curl relaxed.

Now you can start to try some height, so that you're really falling. Begin your rolls from a squatting position, instead of lying on your back, and practice the falls to right and left. Start to swing your arm down as soon as you begin to fall; your arm should hit the mat a fraction of a second before your body does. This is what actually breaks the fall, and helps you to bounce back up again. Remember to keep your head tucked into your chest.

When you've mastered the falls to right and left sides from the squatting position, you're ready to get even more height by gradually straightening your knees at the start. Continue increasing your height from the mat until you can fall to either side from a standing position.

Illus. 84: The backward fall from standing position.

Backward Fall

If you've ever done any tumbling, you may already have mastered this fall. At any rate, you already know the position in which you land on the mat. The backward fall is essentially the same as the falls to the side, except that both arms are used simultaneously to beat down on the mat. Lie on your back on the mat, head and chin tucked into chest, knees drawn up, and arms extended flat on the mat for support. This is the position in which you land.

It will be an easy step to achieve the backward fall next from a sitting position, but not so easy to master it from a full stand. Take your time on this; gradually straighten your knees, getting a little more height with each session. You're doing well if you can perform a good, confident backward fall from a full standing position at the end of two or three weeks of steady practice.

Illus. 85: Concluding the backward fall.

Forward Somersault Fall

Also called the Forward Rolling Fall, this is not exactly the same as the forward somersault in tumbling and gymnastics. For one thing, the object of this fall is not necessarily to land back on your feet. Things move quickly on the judo mat, as they do in real self-defense situations. You can't count on your ability to convert every forward fall into a somersault. What you can usually do, however, is turn it into a break-fall. (All of the various falls are often and correctly called break-falls by judo experts.)

Further, you do not roll directly forward over your head and back in the forward somersault fall; the object is to cushion the fall with the right or left shoulder. Thus, you will be rolling diagonally forward to the right or left.

Assume a squatting position on the mat, resting on the balls of your feet rather than on your heels. Push yourself forward to let

Illus. 86: Starting the forward somersault fall.

your hands down to the mat, palms down. Your hands should be about 18 inches from your toes. You will automatically point yourself in the right direction for a left-shoulder forward fall if you place your left hand in front of your left foot, and your right hand between your feet. Tuck your chin into your chest.

All that remains is to push yourself off your toes, into a rolling diagonal somersault. If you are rolling first to the left, the back of your head should just barely touch the mat—or, even better, not

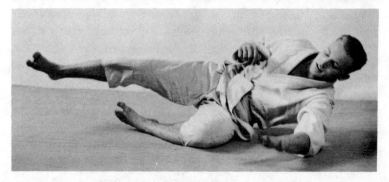

Illus. 87: The end of the forward somersault fall.

touch it at all—with the brunt of the fall being taken by the back of your left shoulder and back.

The forward somersault roll to the diagonal left will bring you across to the right side of your back. Thus, you beat down on the mat with your right arm and hand to break the fall. The situation is reversed, of course, if you take the forward roll to the diagonal right.

Illus. 88: The diagonal end of a forward fall.

When you have mastered this relatively easy forward roll to right and left sides from the squatting position, try it next from a low crouch, and finally from a high crouch. In this last stage, your right foot is placed somewhat forward (if you are rolling to the diagonal right) and your body is bent forward from the waist until both palms are touching the mat in the positions described earlier. Your knees are bent slightly. Your position will now roughly resemble a sprinter's starting crouch, except that your head is tucked in.

Illus. 89: The forward fall from a stand.

Forward Fall from Stand

This is the most difficult of all falls, and is seldom used in actual judo practice or competition. Nevertheless, it may be necessary in self-defense, and is always taught in advanced judo classes. It is also an excellent warm-up exercise. This forward fall is the only one in which you do not go into a curl or somersault.

To achieve it, fall forward from a standing position, bending your body only slightly and breaking the fall with your hands and forearms, as shown above. Your head, body, and knees are thus protected. Note that you do not bend at the knees or waist. Your body is kept straight.

Practice the fall first from a kneeling position. This will help you get accustomed to the idea of breaking your fall with forearms and palms; remember to beat down on the mat with both forearms and hands simultaneously.

Finally, practice the fall from a full standing position. As you tip forward slowly on your toes, the upper half of your body is bent forward in order to achieve a slight convex curve—convex in

Illus. 90: Landing position in the forward fall from stand.

relation to the final position of the body on the ground. (Again, see illustration above.)

Judo masters do not consider themselves expert in performing this fall until they can land successfully after throwing themselves into the air from a short running jump. It is a most impressive stunt in any judo exhibition, but requires a great deal of practice. No beginner should attempt it until he has mastered all the other falls.

10. Ketsugo, Judo and Jiu-Jitsu

Now that you know how to fall, you're ready for self-defense. In this chapter you'll learn some of the most basic and important throws and maneuvers: the shoulder throw, hip throw, side-sweep, somersault throw, arm-lock and throw, and the swinging arm-lock and twist throw. All of these are excellent and effective, and all are potentially dangerous. Use them only when you mean business.

What can you do when somebody stronger grabs you? The second part of this chapter takes up two useful methods of release: the release from three different kinds of wrist-holds, and the release from a choke-hold.

The throws are balance and leverage techniques, and require no great strength, but they take a lot of practice before you can begin to call yourself an expert. And remember: while strength is not *required*, it definitely gives you a great advantage. So you would be wise not to separate body-building and self-defense; they belong together.

PART I—THE THROWS

Shoulder Throw

What do you visualize when you think of judo? If you're like most people, you probably think of the dramatic over-shoulder throw, in which your opponent is thrown or "flipped" over your back. This is one of the most effective maneuvers in self-defense.

There's nothing mysterious or difficult about the throw, and it should be mastered because it's a good defense against a number of attacks. Let's go through it in slow motion.

Facing your partner, grasp his right elbow with your left hand, (see below). Step in close to his body, pivoting around so that you're facing the same direction he is. As you perform the turn, bring your right hand under his right arm, grasping his upper arm close to the shoulder (Illus. 92).

Illus. 91: Shoulder throw, starting position.

Illus 92: Second stage of the shoulder throw.

Now you have a good grip. Pull his right arm forward as you bend your upper body forward, and your partner will be pulled over your right shoulder and back, and down onto the mat (Illus. 93, 94, 95).

An excellent variation of this is to sink down low as you pivot in and around, keeping your knees bent. As you move into the throw, straighten your legs quickly. This alone will lift your partner off the mat, and the forward-bending motion will complete the throw.

Illus. 93: In mid-air in the shoulder throw.

Illus. 94: About to land.

Illus. 95: The landing.

This variation is good, and should be used, when both partners are about the same height. When the other person is considerably taller, use the bending-forward technique alone.

The shoulder throw, like every other move in self-defense, should be practiced until you can do it without thinking about the steps. In the first session, practice the throw slowly, step by step, until you have the idea. Do it that way two or three times. Then reverse positions, and let your partner practice. The one who is being thrown should have no trouble taking this fall on his shoulder and back.

After that, you should be able to perform the throw in a smooth, quick, continuous motion. *Speed is essential.* In a real self-defense situation, of course, nobody waits around for you to get the proper position or the right grip. You may never be able to duplicate exactly the maneuvers you learn in practice, so you should always be ready to improvise.

In the shoulder throw, for example, suppose you can't get a good grip on your opponent's elbow—what then? Simply try to get hold of his sleeve, forearm, or wrist. The general idea is to learn to recognize the basic and important motions in each technique, and practice them with your own variations.

The shoulder throw is extremely effective, and must therefore be practiced with care. There are three rules that should always be observed when you're working with a partner:

1. It goes without saying that both you and your partner should know how to fall. Before attempting the throw, always warm up with a few front falls and forward rolling falls.

2. Always practice this one on a mat.

3. Never let go of your partner. Repeat: *Never let go of your partner*. Hang on tight to his right arm, especially at the height of the throw, and continue to hang on until after he's landed on the mat. Remember that you'll both be practicing the throw, and you'll certainly want him to hang on, too. The one who is doing the throwing can help break his partner's fall by pulling up on his right arm or sleeve as he's about to hit the mat. The partner who is being thrown uses his left arm, shoulder and back to break the fall.

The Hip Throw

One of the most basic, most important, most useful, and most spectacular throws in judo is the hip throw. It is also one of the hardest to learn and master, because most beginners tend to make certain natural mistakes. Don't allow yourself to become discouraged. Get a patient partner or instructor, and practice this on a mat. *Anyone* can learn the throw; and once you've learned it, you can throw almost anyone, regardless of weight or strength.

Therefore, if you find that you are failing to execute the throw properly, never assume that your partner is too heavy, or that you lack sufficient strength. These are natural assumptions among beginners, and they are almost always wrong. Most failures are due to improper placement of feet, and failure to understand the correct action of the hip.

Illus. 96: The start of the hip throw.

Face your opponent, assuming standard posture and grip. Take a short step forward with your right foot, pointing your toes toward the inner side of your opponent's right foot. This means that your own body will turn to the left, beginning the pivot that you will quickly complete. Simultaneously, release your hold on your opponent's left lapel, and slide your right hand and arm around your opponent's waist. As you complete the pivot, you will have your back to opponent, and your body in close contact with his. Note carefully that you do *not* try to step to the outside of your opponent's feet. Correct pivoting action and stance will bring your feet within his. This is your first objective.

Illus. 97: Note the right arm
around opponent's waist
in the hip throw.

The actual throwing is done with the hip as the central pivot. This action, too, must be clearly understood.

First, your hips must be lower than opponent's hips. Unless your opponent is taller, therefore, this means that you must bend your knees. The action of straightening your knees and bending forward, pushing your hips *back* into him, and pulling down on his right sleeve with your left hand, will lift your opponent off the mat. Note that you do not try to lift your opponent *up* with your hips; you drive his hips *back*, and he will be lifted onto your own

Illus. 98: Completing the hip throw.

hips and across your back. Now you continue the pivot, twisting around to the left with your left hip, still pulling down with your left hand. Your opponent will be balanced on and then pulled over your right hip; when you turn further and move away from beneath him, he is unsupported and falls down on the mat.

It is not always necessary or essential to release your opponent's left lapel and slide the right hand around his waist. The standard grip may be retained throughout the throw, and this may increase the surprise value of your attack. However, it is more difficult to learn the throw this way, and you would do well to put your right hand around his waist until you have mastered the basic technique.

Illus. 99: Beginning the side-sweep.

The Side-Sweep

One of the trickiest and most effective throws, the side-sweep is especially good against an opponent who has no knowledge of judo. It can also be used, of course, against another student, but he is much more likely to be expecting it. Against the uninitiated, the side-sweep comes like a bomb out of nowhere—he's being swept through the air before he knows what hit him.

In fact, he may never really know how he was thrown. This is one of the strange, valuable and bewildering effects of certain judo techniques. The gestures, especially in this throw, are smooth and almost gentle, rather than violent. Instead of pushing, you yield—momentarily. Your partner or opponent is continually pushing, and shifting his weight. Then, suddenly, as he is changing his center of balance, your yielding becomes a weapon. In one co-ordinated movement, you actually do three things: pull, push,

Illus. 100: Sweeping opponent's right foot to the left.

and sweep. Yet no strength is needed. It's the sudden loss of balance, not force, that does the trick.

A little practice is necessary to master the sense of timing and coordination of three simultaneous movements. But the practice is well worth it: the side-sweep seldom fails, and can be used very easily against a bigger and stronger opponent.

In this maneuver especially, you must keep your eyes on your opponent's feet. One who is unfamiliar with judo is likely to watch your face, thinking he can read your intentions. Actually, this makes him doubly vulnerable.

Assume standard position and grip: with your left hand grasp the underside of your opponent's right sleeve, and with your right hand grasp his upper left lapel. (During practice, of course, your partner will have the same grip on you.)

As you begin to maneuver and circle about the mat, you yield

Illus. 101: Opponent begins to fall in the side-sweep.

momentarily to your partner's attempts to push you backwards, or to your left side. Wait until he is in the process of shifting his weight forward to his right foot. Your object is to sweep your opponent's right foot to his left side, just before his foot comes down again on the mat.

Contact is made with your opponent's outer right ankle. Turn your left foot—the sweeping foot—in to the side and up, so that the bottom of your foot is hitting your opponent's ankle.

As you perform the sweeping movement, you must simultaneously pull *down* on opponent's right sleeve, and *up* on his left lapel. The sweeping action alone is not always sufficient to throw your opponent, particularly if you have misjudged his balance and distribution of weight.

The side-sweep sounds complicated. Can you really use it on a
bully? Absolutely. It's the ideal throw when you're grappling
with him, or when he grabs you from the front.

Somersault Throw

In judo tournaments, this is considered a sacrifice throw, since
you deliberately choose to risk a backward fall to the mat in order
to execute the somersault throw, sometimes also called the overhead throw.

In self-defense, it is an excellent surprise throw against an
opponent who attempts to grab or push you. First, try to obtain
something close to the standard grip on opponent's right sleeve
and left lapel; or grasp both arms, or both lapels. It is important
that you have a good grip with both hands.

Illus. 103: Falling back for the somersault throw.

As your opponent pushes, you let yourself suddenly sink back and down to the ground, curling into a backward fall, and pulling your opponent forward. The closer you are to your opponent when you begin to fall, the more effectively you can execute this throw. It is difficult to perform at arms' length. Maintain a tight curl as you sit down; try to land just in back of your own left heel.

As you begin to pull your opponent over, bring your right foot up and under your opponent's stomach. The power of your right leg is then used to lift your opponent off the ground and to throw him over your head. The idea is not to *kick* your opponent in the stomach, but to use your foot for a lifting and pushing action.

Use your arms throughout to pull your opponent forward, over,

(Above) Illus. 104: Bringing the right foot up.

Illus. 105: Lifting opponent up.

Illus. 106: The somersault throw completed.

and down. Practice this one only on a mat, and only with a partner who can perform the forward rolling fall.

Finally, this is not a good technique to use if you are much shorter than your partner or opponent.

Arm-Lock and Throw

This is an excellent leverage technique, as popular among FBI and Army Intelligence agents as it is among youngsters learning the rudiments of self-defense. The great value of the arm-lock is that it provides a technique which may be used to restrain and control an opponent who may be annoying or harassing, but not really dangerous. The show-off or bully is put in his place nicely with this technique, which is more humiliating than painful.

Illus. 107: Grasping wrist for arm-lock.

It is not really a judo technique, although it is Oriental. It looks impressively like judo, however, and should in itself be enough to convince anyone that you've been trained in self-defense.

If your opponent's right hand is coming down from above, grasp his wrist with your own right hand so that your palm is turned outward, that is, toward your right side (see above).

If your opponent's hand is reaching for you, or pushing, at chest level, use a normal overhand grip when you grasp his wrist. In order to force his arm to bend upwards, use a chop: strike hard at the inside of his right elbow joint with the outer side of your left palm. (The chop is the kind of blow used in karate.)

Now bring your left hand up in back of your opponent's right arm, between his forearm and biceps, and under his arm to grasp your own right wrist (see page 120). Pulling down on your right

Illus. 108: Left hand comes into action in the arm-lock.

wrist with your left hand and bending forward will easily force your opponent backwards and down. You can now bring him to the ground if necessary. Simple arm pressure will take him down smoothly. Kicking his right leg out from under him with your own leg or thigh will do the job more forcefully.

This is also an excellent defense against a knife attack when the thrust comes from above. Use your right forearm to parry the downward thrust, and capture your opponent's wrist quickly. This takes speed. But speed and accuracy are not matters of luck; they may be developed by constant practice with a partner using a rubber knife.

The arm-locks and wrist-holds especially should be practiced against a left-hand attack.

Illus. 109: The arm-lock and throw fells the opponent.

Illus. 110: Beginning the swinging arm-lock.

Swinging Arm-Lock and Twist-Throw

This throw is another favorite with government agents; it is a technique requiring speedy execution.

Grasp your opponent's wrist with both hands. Swing his arm quickly up and over your head, as you pivot to the left on your left foot (see page 123). Continued twisting pressure on his wrist will force your opponent's body to bend forward and down. Further twisting will bring him to the ground.

Be very careful in practicing this with your partner. Violent twisting will cause considerable pain, and possible injury to his arm.

Like the previous arm-lock, this too may be used as a defense against knife attack. In this case it is useful against an underhand

Illus. 111: Start the swing up.

Illus. 112: Bring opponent's arm way up.

(Left) Illus. 113: Pivot around in the swinging arm-lock.

(Below) Illus. 114: Twist opponent's arm to throw him.

thrust, which must first be parried to the side or met with slashing karate blows to the forearm and elbow joint.

PART II—RELEASES

A stronger adversary may attempt to restrain, pull, or push you by using a tight grip on either or both of your wrists. Releases from wrist-holds are easy to master, and should be learned early. You would do well to practice these until your response is automatic. Releases are good when you're in no real danger, and you don't want to take a chance of hurting your opponent by throwing him.

Release from Wrist-Hold on Both Hands

Twist your hands outward, *always in the direction of your opponent's thumb.*

Illus. 115: Twist hands outward to break wrist-hold.

Illus. 116: The wrist-hold is broken.

If your opponent is considerably stronger, use the following mock-resistance technique: Start to push your hands outward toward your opponent's fingers, as if trying to pull away. Your opponent will resist your movement, and try to pull you in closer. Then snap your hands quickly in and upwards, twisting toward your opponent's thumbs. This will break the hold.

Release from Single-Hand-Hold on One Hand

This is the easiest release, and uses the same basic technique as above. Twist your hand away in direction of your opponent's thumb. This is a basic leverage technique, well known to lifeguards, who must be able to release themselves quickly from the desperate, clinging grip of panicky swimmers.

(Above) Illus. 117: Twist toward opponent's thumb in this hold.

Illus. 118: The release comes easily.

Illus. 119: The hold is tight.

Release from Two-Hand-Hold on One Wrist

In this situation your opponent has one of your wrists captured with a combination overhand-underhand grip. Reach down between his hands to grasp your own hand, without interlocking your fingers. Bend your knees, keep your elbows tucked in close to body. Straighten your knees with a snap; use your arm, shoulder, and body strength to bring your clasped hands up and out quickly and powerfully, in an uppercut motion. (With luck, you may connect.)

Again, if your opponent is too strong for this, use the mock-resistance technique. Instead of pulling away, use your free hand to grasp your own hand, and push down until your opponent begins to pull up. Then help him: pull up harder and faster than he expects.

(Above) Illus. 120: Grasp your own hand.

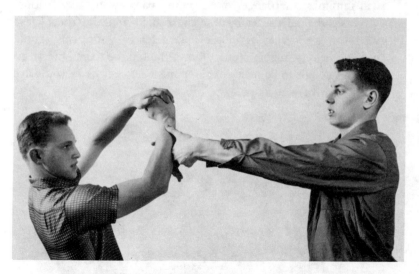

Illus. 121: An uppercut breaks the hold.

Illus. 122: The choke-hold.

Release from Choke-Holds

Defenses against choke-holds are even more important than wrist-hold releases, and should be learned and mastered early. A choke is always a frightening hold. The automatic response will minimize the danger of becoming panicky in this situation.

This is the defense against the choke-hold from the front: Clasp your hands together as in previous defense. Your arms should not be held straight. Your elbows should be bent and arms spread enough to contact your opponent's forearms as you drive up hard with your arms.

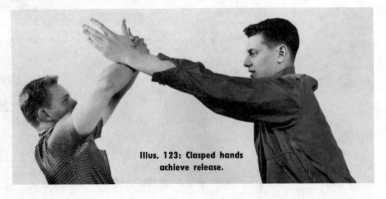

Illus. 123: Clasped hands achieve release.

Against the choke from behind, the best defense is a scraping kick to the shins. Never try to pull forward from a choke from behind. If necessary, throw yourself backward, falling on top of your opponent or butting his face with the back of your head. These measures are as extreme as they sound; the choke from behind requires extreme action. Do not attempt to practice these techniques. They are employed only in actual self-defense situations.

Illus. 124: A scraping kick to the shins is the best defense against the choke from behind.

11. Serious Business

Many books on self-defense describe a number of pretty maneuvers designed to protect you from knife attacks and gun threats, and teach you how to disarm your opponent. We have already considered two such techniques in the section on arm-locks.

It is true that you can develop speed and power and accuracy. It is true that you might, with luck and constant practice, defend yourself against a weapon attack, and even disarm and subdue your opponent.

There is another possibility, however: you might not. It is only in the movies that the good guy always wins.

If you meet someone who is armed, *don't play hero*. You should be more interested in staying alive than in saving your money or getting a medal. How you react will depend on the kind of threat; but the following suggestions are based on the assumption that your main purpose in life is to stay around and enjoy it.

First: Do anything you can to avoid getting hurt. It may mean running away from a man with a knife; it may mean handing your wallet over to a man with a gun. If you can avoid danger and injury by giving in—then give in.

Second: If the assailant is not interested in your money or valuables, and you have no chance to escape, then you would be justified in using any technique, and all your physical power, to defend yourself.

Defense against a Knife Attack

Close contact with an opponent wielding a gun, knife, or club, then, should be considered a desperate last resort. If you must defend yourself, use your feet first. It is better to kick out at a man holding a knife or broken bottle than to attempt a defense with your bare hands. You can deliver more power with your feet; the points of your shoes and your heels can be deadly weapons. Even a boy or girl has enough kicking power to splinter a knee-cap or break a leg.

Violent methods? Of course; there is no way around them. An opponent armed with a knife, broken bottle, or club must be considered deadly. He may be a killer, a lunatic, a violent drunk, a member of a cold-blooded or vicious street gang, a crazed and desperate drug-addict—or a combination of any of those. Your obligation is to protect and defend yourself, and any friend or loved one with you.

Defense against a Gun

If you are confronted by an assailant carrying a gun, and the intent is clearly robbery, *take no chances*. It is better to lose 100% of your money than take a 1% chance of losing your life. Further, you might endanger the lives of others.

If intent is *not* robbery: See section on street-fighting defense that follows.

Common Sense in Self-Defense

On this subject, there happens to be an old Chinese saying: "Don't shoot a sparrow with a cannon." If you're just fooling around with another good-natured guy, you certainly wouldn't want to use a painful hold or a dangerous judo throw. But as a beginning self-defense expert, you have an even more serious obligation as a gentleman and as a person of honor. Self-defense training arms you with knowledge that can be dangerous. It is a weapon, but it is not enough to say that the weapon should be used only for defense. We must say further that it is up to you to gauge the seriousness of the situation, and to use just enough of your technique to gain control.

Never attempt a throw that can inflict serious injury if a restraining hold is all that is necessary. Never kick, chop, or slash except in the most extreme and threatening circumstances.

It is not always easy to decide on the spur of the moment just what is called for. And of course it is more difficult for the beginner than for the expert, since the beginner's experience and knowledge of a variety of techniques are limited. There is really only one sound answer: Try to continue learning. Practice whenever you can. Join a judo club, if possible. Sport judo can be a wonderful, lifelong hobby.

The more you learn, and the more skillful you become, the more confident you will be of your physical adequacy and your ability to defend yourself. The more capable you will be, too, of using the right technique at the right time.

It is not easy to have compassion for a wise guy or a blustering bully, but remember that he is almost sure to be an insecure person, with far less courage and substance than you or the average person. Don't let him push you around; don't baby him; and if you must parry or throw a punch, do it without hesitation. But it probably won't be necessary to injure him, either. Try to use control, and keep your wits about you. Depend upon it: the bully will back down from a show of confidence and ability.

Street-Fighting Defense

We have granted the wisdom of the ancient Chinese, and acknowledged that it is not necessary to shoot a sparrow with a cannon. But one of the laws of quotesmanship is that for every ancient proverb, there is an equal and opposite ancient proverb. So we ask: who ever heard of a street-fight in a rice paddy? This provocative question brings us round to a solid American proverb: you can't stop a lion with a B-B gun.

If you are ever confronted by members of a vicious street gang, or experienced "dirty fighters," you must realize that there is no longer a question of which techniques to use or not to use. You cannot afford to assume that you are dealing with regular bullies. Certain kinds of people actually thrive on physical violence of the lowest and dirtiest sort. Further, they may be armed with switchblades, home-made blackjacks, "zip-guns," or lengths of metal pipe.

You would be foolish to come into close contact with such a gang if you can possibly avoid it. They may not be after your money or valuables, but simply "out for kicks"—violent physical ones. If you are a good runner and can get away by running, then *this is the time to run*. It is not the time to be a hero. Ignore remarks and insults; if you are not surrounded, just keep walking fast. If you can scare off a threatening gang by shouting for help, then do that.

The following remarks apply only if you are surrounded and actually threatened with direct attack:

In the section on defense against knife attack, we said it was better to kick out than try to get close to your adversary. Kicking may be considered a "dirty" method of fighting, but it is also a very effective method, and this is the time to use it. You cannot use lollipop techniques in a critical self-defense situation.

Actually, kicking in self-defense is a highly developed art which originated in France, and is known as *savate*. Books have been written on that method alone; it takes practice to master all the forms. But basically savate is kicking, and you can do it with your heel, toe, sides, and bottom of your foot from different striking positions. You already know that you can deliver a great deal more striking power with your feet and legs than with your arms. However, remember that care must be taken to keep your weight and the center of balance over your supporting foot, while striking out with the other. Bend your supporting knee for better balance, and your body can usually be bent and crouched away from your opponent.

A kick at the knee-cap, for example, is not delivered like a football kick, toes forward, but like a push. (See illustration.)

Illus. 125: A savate kick to the knee. Keep your balance over your supporting leg.

The French method of savate is also incorporated in the Oriental karate, and partly in jiu-jitsu. For taming the bully, controlling the annoying show-off, and in most other self-defense situations, you will not need to resort to kicking. When the circumstances are critical, however, its value should be acknowledged, and then you should use the kick without hesitating.

GIVE A YELL!

You've heard the old football cheer: "Give a yell! Give a yell! Give a good substantial yell!" In a fight, too, yelling makes good substantial sense, because we know now that it adds more than spirit. Yelling can make you stronger!

Sound crazy? It's true. Scientists who have studied the phenomenon of yelling have found that it actually helps you muster more muscle strength than you think you have. Most people don't use their full strength. Shouting and general noise-making can make you stronger by 15 or 20 per cent. (Lifting a heavy box, for example, will be easier if you grunt and groan while you're lifting.)

In a fight, yelling can have a tremendous effect. It's hard to measure, of course, but it could mean the difference between winning and losing. Self-defense experts, fighters, and warriors have known about this for a long time. Think of the Indian warcries, the whooping and yelling; think of the shouting in a cavalry charge.

Shouting not only increases your own physical strength and confidence—it also frightens your opponent. It can paralyze him with fear. In World War II, the Japanese came charging across the battlefields yelling "Banzai!" As small as they were, they gained a reputation for being fighting madmen.

Shouting, in karate, is sometimes called the "ki-ya yell." *What* you yell doesn't matter, as long as you make plenty of noise.

So, if you must attack—do it with a yell! The wilder and louder the better! Scream! Twist your face! Sound off! Put on a good act —it can give you the upper hand.

After all this violent activity, our little book comes crunching to a close. Needless to say, I hope you will never have to use the techniques described in this last chapter.

If you think of self-defense training as a sport activity, and don't worry too much about meeting with danger, I think you will find it a most enjoyable form of athletics—gymnastics, if you will, with a useful purpose. If you are working on weight-lifting and body-building, this will keep you limber.

No matter which exercises you choose, I think you will find that body-building is a pleasant, healthy and satisfying way to keep in good physical shape. Work on these two activities together, and you'll be unbeatable. Along with your new-found muscles and self-defense skill, your self-confidence will shoot up quickly.

Remember: just *reading* this book will not make you an expert. You can't get anywhere in body-building or self-defense without regular practice. You have to get the feel of the throws, understand balance, learn to move fast.

Think of how many times you've said to yourself, "I'm going to start a regular program soon." "Soon" is now. Now is the time to begin your physical training. You can have the kind of body you've always day-dreamed about. You can have the skill and confidence of the self-defense expert. You can; there's no question about it.

All you have to do is start now.

PART II

karate

This section emphasizes the purely amateur nature of the sport of Karate. Here, the author stresses basic principles and presents each technique in turn. When a student takes instruction in Karate, he soon sees positive effects, not only in his physique, but in his intellectual abilities as well.

The Technique of Karate

"Karate, an art of fighting that originated in China, uses all of the limbs of the body for defence and attack." This statement tells in a few words the essence of a competitive sport from the Orient, a sport that is extremely varied and is becoming increasingly well known.

Karate (pronounced "kah-rah-teh"), in reality, is not as simple and uncomplicated as this statement. On the contrary, every Karate teacher finds again and again that his beginning students lose perspective and begin to despair because of the many techniques they must learn. In this book will be offered some new methods and aids, especially for the teacher. Certain mechanical and psychological laws are important to know before you can understand the technique of Karate. It is also possible for the student himself to understand the technique of Karate once he achieves the correct point of view.

By study, you will discover similarities and relationships again and again between various techniques. Eventually the technique of Karate as a whole will then no longer appear to be a collection of various techniques. Once a person understands the entire technique of Karate, he gets a complete "overview," and the whole area no longer seems large and difficult to survey. Moreover, any technique of Karate which was not known to you before, no longer seems to be completely "new." You understand it because it is subject to the same principles that you have already been working to understand. Therefore, the first prerequisite for learning Karate is *correct understanding*.

Practice is useful only after you understand the technique of Karate being demonstrated. The prerequisite for understanding is *exact observation* of the technique being demonstrated or exact reading of the instruction book. This brings up another very important point. Understanding a technique alone is not sufficient. You must be able to make the technique your very own, and this comes through *practice*.

It can very well happen that someone has understood a technique, practices it all the time, and in spite of this, does not

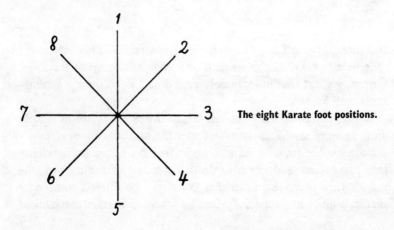

The eight Karate foot positions.

succeed in mastering perfect technique. *Self-criticism* or critical self-observation is lacking. You know how a technique should look. So, you very critically observe yourself doing it. You improve on it, work on it. You look critically again and again. How is *kokutsu-dachi* (the back stance) supposed to look, and how does it look when I do it? You have to compare and see what is wrong with your performance and then correct it. By practicing this way, with understanding and self-criticism, you have a great advantage over the person who practices, say, three hours every day, but has not understood the techniques and does not know what he is doing wrong.

For that reason, the phrase "less is more," when correctly understood, is valid for Karate. Ten jabs with the fist every day practiced with understanding and self-criticism (in front of a mirror) can be more valuable than hours of thrusting back and forth like a robot while understanding is lacking.

No one can promise that you will master Karate in a short time. But that is no excuse for not practicing with understanding and self-criticism, and then practicing again and again.

In summing up, here are the prerequisites for learning Karate:
1. Exact observation and concentration.
2. Understanding.
3. Practice, while
4. Observing yourself critically.

These are the prerequisites for learning the *technique* of Karate. However, Karate does not consist only of technique. The second part of this book treats the philosophical side in great detail, but in this first part we are concerned with technique alone.

Body tension

Karate is a competitive sport in which the concentrated force of your body is pressed for a short moment at some point of your opponent's body for the purpose of defence or attack. Expressed in another way, it is control of the tension of your body at the right moment—the muscles are tensed only for a short moment, the moment of striking, then are immediately relaxed again. Your body at the moment of striking stands there behind the technique as hard as a block of granite.

The tenser the muscles of your body are during this short moment, the better. During this extremely short instant, there must be no weak spot in your body. The technique must be perfected while the "substructure" is solid. The peaks of tension in position and in striking must occur simultaneously for the techniques to have a great shock effect.

You must be able to move swiftly and gracefully in Karate, and fast graceful movements are possible only when you are relaxed. Therefore, the tensing must be only a very short term thing. However, it is the decisive thing in Karate, for without it Karate would be just an acrobatic dance with soft, supple movements.

You have to be able to combine the hard with the soft—a goal that you can achieve only after long years of intensive study. The old Chinese masters laughed at anyone who tried only to introduce

Illus. 1. Normal breathing. It is easy for your partner to lift you up.

Illus. 2. Breathing from the diaphragm. By concentrating on the hara, you will stick to the floor.

strength into his techniques, for a true master combines the soft and the hard. He is neither soft nor hard, but rather both at the same moment. This sentence from a book on gymnastics is valid: "Whoever is master of relaxation (intellectually and spiritually as well) is also master of tension." The key to this ability of being both hard and soft at the same time (and combining them) lies in the *hara*, which can be practiced very consciously. However, more about that later.

The low stance

The lower you stand, the greater the security of your stance, for the surface of your stance is greater and your center of gravity is lowered. The fact of the matter is that your defence or attack technique will be that much more effective the better the security of your stance. In addition, your low stance supplies tension in your bent legs (as in a drawn bow) which you can apply in a flash to attack or withdraw quickly. However, to extract the greatest measure of effectiveness, something else is also important.

The direction of the tension

All positions in Karate are thought out to give them the maximum effect for a particular purpose (whether attack or defence, to the rear or to the side). Expressed differently, the position makes it possible to let the concentrated tension of your body become highly effective during defence and attack in whatever direction is necessary.

The technical significance of "hara"

The literal translation of *hara* means "stomach," but in the figurative sense it indicates the true center of gravity of a person, the very middle. We will discuss the figurative sense of *hara* in detail in the second half of this book. At this point we merely want to discuss its technical meaning very briefly. There is an old Chinese saying, "Before you can learn to conquer others, you must first learn to stand well." Whoever loses his balance is weak. He cannot defend himself or attack effectively. In order to maintain your equilibrium, you must concentrate on the center of your body, your center of gravity, your *hara*. Here, in the significance of *hara*, Karate has the same basis as Judo or Aikido.

Whatever the position connected with a technique, the force from the *hara* must be concentrated at one point. Always think consciously of the fact that the strength for every technique comes from the *hara*.

So as not to get your midpoint out of balance, so that all action can start forcefully and effectively from the center of your body, it is important to hold yourself erect. Keep your body in each of your Karate positions and actions so that your navel always points up slightly.

A good exercise of *hara* is breathing with your diaphragm. This type of breathing is practiced consciously by the masters of Judo and especially by practitioners of Aikido. The inhaled air is pressed down, and breathing is done not so much by lifting and releasing the chest as by moving the diaphragm up and down. By breathing this way, you can lower your center of gravity somewhat. This means that although you are standing on the same surface area, the security of your stance is greater.

This is valid to the same extent for Karate, Judo, and Aikido. The significance of the *hara* is that it is the center of gravity and at the same time the center of equilibrium of the body. "Whoever loses his balance cannot bring technique into play and is already half beaten."

Breathing

Correct breathing is more important than anything else in Karate. In Karate you must master body tension, you must concentrate your strength at a certain moment, and in order to obtain the highest measure of effectiveness, you must breathe very consciously.

Inhaling makes relaxation easier; exhaling helps you when tensing. Various systems of gymnastics are based on this fact. As far as Karate is concerned, this means that you exhale at the moment you develop your greatest force, and you do this quickly, like an explosion!

In Karate you often see opponents using force while holding

their breath. Many Judokas also hold their breath at the moment of the greatest development of strength (at the beginning of a throw). However, from a medical viewpoint, this is usually considered unhealthy. In addition, it is not very efficient. We know today, after an extensive series of experiments carried out by sports physicians and physiologists that the greatest force is developed at the point when half the air in the lungs has been expelled. You must have at some time experienced this fact yourself. For example, you may have had to lift a heavy object from the floor to the table. You take hold of it, but it is so heavy you can hardly lift it from the ground. What do you do? You tense all your muscles, you exert yourself and involuntarily you gasp—you inhale deeply, and then you exhale. All of a sudden you can lift it up quickly. In the course of doing this, you exhaled part of the air that you were previously compressing, and in doing this you helped your muscles to tense. This is the main reason for uttering the battle cry of Karate, "KIAI," which helps to attain your maximal body tension at the moment of striking.

The hip is the point of origin of every total movement

The basic principle for every total movement is: Hip first—limbs afterwards.

We will encounter this principle again and again in every technique.

Illus. 3. The natural and relaxed stance of the hachiji-dachi.

1. Stances and Movements

The positions and movements of Karate differ essentially from those of everyday life. In Karate, your body always moves as a whole with your hip (more exactly, the *hara*) as the center point. Your leg does not proceed and your body follow after, but rather every movement is a unity, originating and determined by the center of gravity and force of the body, the *hara*. The following "tests" will show you whether your movements are suitable for Karate, i.e., whether they start from the *hara*.

Illus. 4 (left). The basic stance, hachiji-dachi, from which you can move easily into one of the low, tensed positions, such as kiba-dachi (below).

Illus. 5a. Kiba-dachi position of the feet and knees.

Illus. 5b. Kiba-dachi stance.

Hachiji-dachi, the basic stance

Body relaxed and natural (Illus. 3 and 4). This stance leaves all possibilities and directions open. From this position, you can slide into one of the low, tensed positions, for example, into *kiba-dachi*.

Kiba-dachi, the straddle-leg stance

This position is particularly strong at the sides. Your feet are spread apart twice the breadth of your shoulders, your toes pointing slightly to the inside. The weight of your body is distributed evenly, and your knees are pressed to the outside (Illus. 5 and 6). In this way, your position becomes solid and contains a great supply of tension. Keep the upper part of your body erect. Breathe with your diaphragm. Push your hips forward.

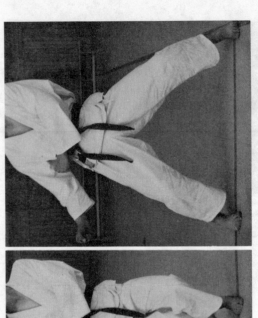

Illus. 7. Glide from kiba-dachi to right.

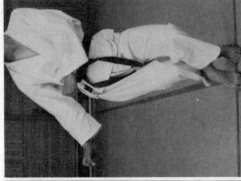

Illus. 8. Legs crossed for a split second.

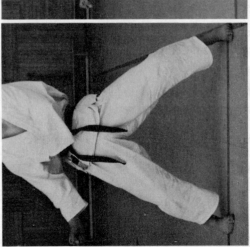

Illus. 9. End in kiba-dachi stance again.

Illus. 6. Kiba-dachi.

Cross-over side movement in kiba-dachi

Let's see how you would move sideways from the *kiba-dachi* stance, for example, to your right (Illus. 7 to 9). The important thing is to be relaxed and glide! Do not bend your hips, but bend your supporting (right) leg, and cross your left foot in front of it.

During all movements from this and other Karate positions, imagine that a low ceiling is just above your head. Tense all your muscles briefly at the moment you have spread and placed your right leg down in its final position. Press both knees to the outside at the same time and tense your abdomen (breathing through your diaphragm). By doing this, you will immediately stand sure and solid.

180-degree turn

For a pivot on your left foot, draw up your right foot to cross close behind the left, so that the center of gravity moves along evenly. Only when your right leg touches your supporting (left) leg do you turn your body 180 degrees. Your supporting leg should

In the 180-degree turn, you pivot on your left foot, and bring your right foot past it in a straight line.

remain markedly flexed, and this will help fling the other leg far to the side (Illus. 10 and 11). By forcefully turning on your hip, you use the supply of tension in your bent supporting leg, and this makes the movement rapid and full of power. Tense all muscles for a moment and breathe with your abdominal wall abruptly exhaling.

For practice

From the *hachiji-dachi* (basic) stance, go into *kiba-dachi*, then move at a right angle to the front and to the rear, to the left and to the right. Practice sharp turning of your hip and tensing of your abdominal wall.

Here is a little test which will reveal whether you are able already to move in a way suitable for Karate, whether your movements proceed from the *hara* or from the limbs.

Your partner takes a strong stanglehold on your neck from the front (Illus. 12). You draw up your chin, hold your shoulders high, tense your neck muscles. If you now were to take a step to the side (either leg first), it would be an easy matter for him to throw you down in a second (for you would then be standing momentarilv on one leg).

However, it is possible to escape this hold merely by a true Karate movement into *kiba-dachi*, the straddle-leg stance.

When your opponent has a stranglehold on you, glide back as quick as lightning into a low *kiba-dachi* at right angles. Turn your hip in sharply. Remain erect and tense your abdominal wall. Your opponent will loosen his grip and be pulled off balance (Illus. 13). If you carry out this movement with forceful unity, your opponent will have no opportunity to throw you down. Practice with strong opponents, and don't give up until you can pass this test, even with hefty stranglehold attacks.

Illus. 12   Illus. 13

Getting away from a strangle on your neck.

Zenkutsu-dachi, the forward stance

This is an extremely strong front position. It is used in defending against attacks from the front and particularly for attacking and counter-attacking to the front.

Illus. 14
                                                         Illus. 15
The forward stance, zenkutsu-dachi, from which you can defend easily by turning
away.

Take a stance with your left foot extended two shoulder breadths
forward and out (Illus. 14, 15, 16a, 16b). Your front leg carries
60 per cent of your body weight, your rear leg 40 per cent. Your
rear leg must be completely extended with your knee straight and
your toes pointed as far as possible to the front. Your heels remain
flat on the floor.

From side to side, your feet are a shoulder breadth apart, with
your front toes turned in slightly.

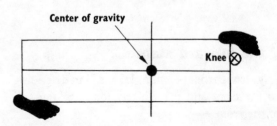

Illus. 16a. The foot and
knee positions in
zenkutsu-dachi.

From the hachiji-dachi stance (Illus. 17, left) make a small arc with your right foot (Illus. 18, right) as you move forwards into the zenkutsu-dachi.

Your body can now be directed to the front in the *zenkutsu-dachi* stance, or it can be turned away. Particularly in defending, you want to turn away in order to give your opponent as little surface area to attack as possible.

Going into the zenkutsu-dachi stance from hachiji-dachi

Step forward with your right foot, making a small arc from the inside outwards. Let your sole glide close to the floor (Illus. 17 and 18). Remember that your body proceeds as a unit with your hip as the central point. Tense all your muscles momentarily as

Illus. 16b. In the zenkutsu-dachi, your front leg must carry 60 per cent of your body weight.

Illus. 19. From the basic hachiji-dachi, glide backwards with your right foot in an arc. Keep your sole parallel to and close to the floor, and leave 60 per cent of your weight on your forward leg.

you place your foot down. Tense your abdominal wall and stand straight.

In stepping backwards with your right foot in an arc from *hachiji-dachi* leave your weight on your front leg. At the same time, bend this supporting leg markedly and shove your left hip to the front (Illus. 19). Your navel must point slightly upwards. Extend your right leg markedly to the rear.

Illus. 20 (left). From the zenkutsu-dachi with left foot forward, you can move in one giant step to zenkutsu-dachi with right foot forward (Illus. 21).

Illus. 22 **Illus. 23** **Illus. 24**

Pass your forward-moving leg very close to your supporting leg and bend low.

If you combine the backward and forward movements of the same leg, you can make a giant step (Illus. 20 and 21 and 22 to 24).

From the rear your right leg goes past your left leg very closely. Keep your supporting leg (left) sharply bent. (Think of the low ceiling over your head!)

The supply of tension in your supporting leg (in this case, the left) enables you to catapult your body correctly to the front. To be sure of accomplishing this, slant your bent supporting leg abruptly forward as soon as your advancing leg has passed the supporting leg. Move your right hip forward. As you place your right leg down, tense all the muscles of your body briefly. Then you will immediately be standing securely and solidly. Proceed continuously in this *zenkutsu-dachi* (forward) stance.

Practice this forward catapulting of your body. You should be conscious of the fact that it is the strength, the supply of tension, in your bent supporting leg which catapults you so rapidly forward. While you are practicing this giant forward step, which you will be using when attacking, think also of your rear leg, which you must *thrust out energetically and forcefully*. Try to speed it forward faster and faster. Always utilize completely the force of

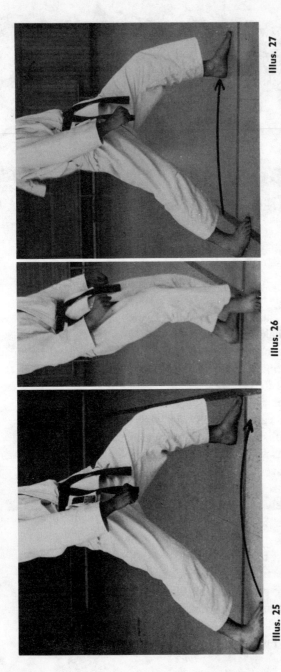

Illus. 25

Illus. 26

Illus. 27

From this giant step forward you start from the zenkutsu-dachi by bringing up your right foot, and in the same forward movement you energetically advance your left foot. Your feet are in the same zenkutsu-dachi position at the finish, but two big lengths forward.

tension in your bent leg. Your Karate movements must be as explosive as a panther's. Animals crouch when getting ready to spring, and in doing so gather the maximum supply of tension. You too must tense at the right moment before speeding forward.

The same principle of catapulting with the aid of a bent supporting leg is also valid for transition into the sideways movements of *kiba-dachi*. Think this over, and attempt catapulting when you practice *kiba-dachi*.

Also practice the giant step backwards. It is like continuous walking, going backwards in the *zenkutsu-dachi*.

Transition forward into zenkutsu-dachi

This is similar to the transition into *kiba-dachi* in that you must change supporting legs. In this instance too, you catapult yourself as you bring up your right foot (Illus. 25) and while you are doing it (Illus. 26), you continue the catapulting force by bringing your left leg up energetically (Illus. 27). You end in the same position of feet but a giant step forward.

Turns in the zenkutsu-dachi stance

In competition, self-defence and in exhibitions (the *kata*), you

Illus. 28   **Illus. 29**
The 180-degree turn on the spot in zenkutsu-dachi is achieved by a simple ankle pivot.

159

need to know how to turn in this position. You will use turns mostly in attacking and counter-attacking.

For a 180-degree turn on the spot, feel out with the balls of your feet. Then turn your body around quickly and forcefully, pivoting on the balls of your feet with the weight of your body simultaneously displaced to the new supporting leg (right leg, in Illus. 28 and 29). Stay erect, right hip forward, tense your abdominal wall as you pivot.

Illus. 30   **Illus. 31**
The 180-degree body turn must be made quickly. Move your right foot in a straight line past your supporting leg and ankle, with your knees remaining bent.

For a 180-degree turn with a large step, your center of gravity, as with all movements in Karate, must remain low. In this case, too, feel out with the balls of your feet, then turn your body quickly, moving your right foot (Illus. 30 and 31) in a straight line past your left (rear) foot. Make certain that you execute the turning of your body as a unity. In this way you will perform certain quick turns for the kata.

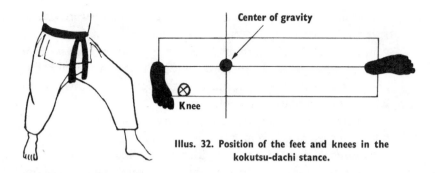

Center of gravity

Knee

Illus. 32. Position of the feet and knees in the kokutsu-dachi stance.

Kokutsu-dachi, the back stance

Have 70 per cent of the weight of your body on your rear leg, 30 per cent on your front leg (Illus. 32). Your right leg, as in *kiba-dachi* (the straddle-leg stance), is turned slightly to the inside and sharply bent at the knee with tension to the outside. Your heels are in a straight line (Illus. 33). *Kokutsu-dachi* is used almost exclusively in defence.

Illus. 33. In the kokutsu-dachi, the main portion of your weight must be on your rear leg. This is a defensive position.

For practice, move forwards and backwards with *kokutsu-dachi*. It is also important to stay erect, keep your hip forward, and tense your abdominal wall. Turns and steps are possible in *kokutsu-dachi* as in *zenkutsu-dachi*, the forward stance. There is a special possibility here—the 180-degree turn on the spot can be made with your feet remaining on a single line.

Practice all positions, especially the transitions from one to the other—for example, from *kiba-dachi* without moving a step into *kokutsu-dachi* and from that position into *zenkutsu-dachi*, and so on, merely by displacement of weight, turning on the balls of your feet or your heels.

For all movements in all positions, it is always valid to think of the leg behind you, and concentrate on keeping tension there.

Position of the body

Karate is mastery of equilibrium. For that reason, with few exceptions, you do not bend your body backwards. Your spine must always remain straight. You may of course turn your body to the side in order to present as little surface area as possible for your opponent to attack. You turn your body to the side especially for defence, and also to transform the power of simultaneously counter-turning for the counter-attack.

Now that we have looked at the "substructures" which help to make techniques as effective as possible, let's turn to the techniques themselves.

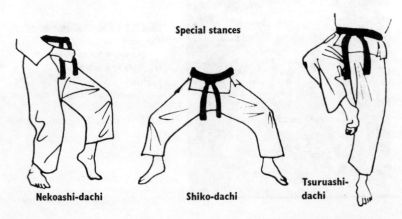

Special stances

Nekoashi-dachi   Shiko-dachi   Tsuruashi-dachi

Survey of the Techniques

Attack Techniques
  Punching technique (*zuki-waza*)
  Striking technique (*uchi-waza*)
  Kicking technique (*keri-waza*)
  Other (attacks with the head, shoulder, and so on)

Blocking techniques (uke-waza)

You can defend yourself first with your arms and then with your legs. It is advisable to stick to this system and this succession. Frequently, one technique results from the other. If you recognize the common factors, your survey over the whole area of Karate is facilitated. You learn more economically.

Many people imitate advanced learners when they see their free movements. Remember that these advanced learners are able to move with agility because they have studied the basic techniques seriously and learned them correctly. Imitation of advanced students without study and practice yourself can be dangerous for the beginner.

Everyone who wishes to master Karate techniques must practice industriously, and study the basic techniques with understanding and self-criticism. One of the paths is patience.

Other basic stances

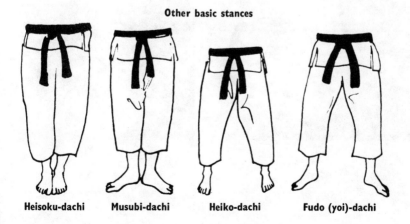

Heisoku-dachi   Musubi-dachi   Heiko-dachi   Fudo (yoi)-dachi

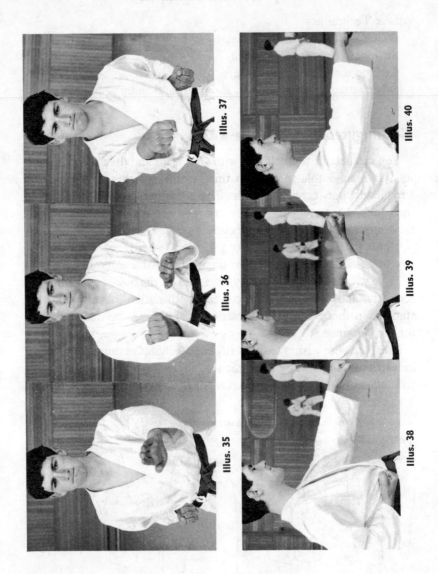

Illus. 35   Illus. 36   Illus. 37

Illus. 38   Illus. 39   Illus. 40

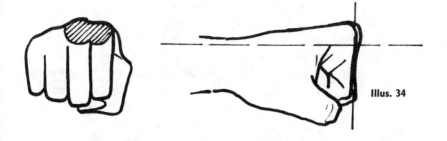

Illus. 34

2. Punching Techniques
(Zuki-waza)

A straight line is the shortest distance between two points. All techniques which steer a straight path to their goal belong to the technique called *seiken-choku-zuki*, the straight thrust with the front of the fist. Illus. 35–37 and 38–40 show how the right fist is cocked, and then thrust forward sharply from the hip. Starting out from the hip with palm up, the fist strikes with palm down, and the wrist tensed.

Position of the fist: Only the knuckles of the index and middle fingers strike the surface (Illus. 34). The fist must extend straight from the wrist so that it does not bend over when it strikes.

Relax your shoulders and sink down. Hold your punching fist palm up so close to your hip that your little finger touches the hip bone and your elbow is pressed to the rear (Illus. 35). Your other hand is extended loosely at a point in front of the center of your body (Illus. 38).

Imagine two lines from your hip bone. One originates at the end of your right pelvic bone and extends to the point in front of your body where your left hand now is. The other originates at your left pelvic bone and extends to the same point.

The punching right fist now advances along the first line, while the left hand recedes smoothly at the same speed back to a fist position along the other line. Just at the instant when the punching right fist is right up front and your left fist is back at your left hip, both fists turn and engage. The right fist turns palm down and the left palm up, ready for the next blow to start. That is the moment to tense your body. To help tensing, exhale at this instant and tense your abdominal wall. Concentrate on your *hara*. The thrust does not come out of your shoulders, but from the middle of your body, from the *hara*. Therefore, be sure you do not let your shoulder go forward.

When you have mastered this fist manoeuvre you will have learned a great part of Karate technique. For that reason, practice it continuously. Just as a master of Judo practices falling before each training session, you practice jabbing with the fist.

Practice this way for each training session, starting from the *hachiji-dachi* (basic stance):

First punch back and forth, slowly and without force, while (a) making sure your elbows brush along your body and that the two straight lines are maintained; then (b) engaging by a synchronized turning of both fists into the final position.

Second, continue to punch slowly, but then tense all your muscles as you turn your fists. All your muscles! For one second. Maintain this tension especially in the side muscles and the abdominal muscles.

Breathing: Breathe in (relaxed), press the air down and punch slowly as you are doing this. Instead of just turning both fists, twist them into final positions, tensing all muscles and exhaling. Then breathe in again, relax, and jab with the other fist.

Now, practice rapid thrusts, 10 with the right hand, then 10 with the left. Do not concentrate on the punching hand, but on the one that is receding. Become conscious of the fact that the receding hand determines the speed of the punching fist. If you concentrate on this, then it will become fact, and will be a great help in increasing speed and bringing your body into tension.

Finally, practice rapid punches alternately with the right and left from *kiba-dachi*, the straddle-leg stance.

Practice the fist punch (*sei-ken*) in this form throughout every training session. As we will see next, the punch with the front of the fist is used in various ways.

Illus. 41   **Illus. 42**   **Illus. 43**

As you advance a giant step, you punch with your fist and catapult forwards. This is the oi-zuki. Advancing leg and fist are on the same side of your body.

The oi-zuki, the lunge punch, same side

With this blow, the punching fist is on the same side of the body as the advancing leg.

Use the catapult-like giant step forward here. The fist strikes at exactly the same moment that the front leg touches down. This technique is highly effective when the high points of tension in your legs and the upper part of your body are simultaneous. Not only the upper part of your body, but your substructure must be stiffly tensed at the moment of striking. This occurs through the *hara*, by stiffening of the abdominal muscles and breathing.

The *oi-zuki* receives its greatest power from the forward movement of your body. For that reason, practice the catapult-like step forward again and again. Let your body shoot forward.

Extend your supporting leg energetically. Start your punching fist from your hip at the very moment when your rear leg passes the supporting leg. Your body will therefore fly forward almost as fast as your fist. Make sure the shoulder of your punching arm is not pushed forward. Do not thrust from your shoulder, but from your *hara*. Practice this punch with the giant step or from *hachiji-dachi*. Aim it principally for the solar plexus and the face.

Illus. 44. Beginners practicing the first stage of the gyaku-zuki.

The gyaku-zuki, the reverse punch

In this punch, if the left leg is in front, the punch is made from the right, and vice versa. Therefore the designation, *gyaku*, meaning reversed.

The force for this punch which is more powerful than the *oi-zuki*, comes from a powerful turning of the hip. To be sure, it is not so fast or so direct as the *oi-zuki*. For this reason and others, it is generally used in counter-attacking.

Basically, one can say that the *oi-zuki* (the same-side form) is faster and more direct. With it, you can use every arm technique quickly and directly, so it is good for attack.

While you can use every arm technique in the *gyaku-zuki* (the reverse form), it is preferred for counter-attacking, mainly because of the sharp turning in of the hip.

Illus. 45   Illus. 46

In the gyaku-zuki, the punch does not start until the front leg has touched down
and you are in the zenkutsu-dachi position.

These two forms are so basic that we must describe them more
thoroughly.

The movement of the *gyaku-zuki* is somewhat more difficult
than that of the *oi-zuki*. As for time, it takes somewhat longer. In
the *gyaku-zuki*, the fist does not strike at the same moment that
the front leg touches down—it does not even start until this
moment (Illus. 45 and 46). It starts too from a position in which
the body is turned 45 degrees away, which you normally take
when defending. The advantage of the *gyaku-zuki* is that you
employ it without loss of time, and turn a defence into counter-
attack. This is valid for all *gyaku* forms.

Analyzing the gyaku-zuki

The *gyaku-zuki* consists of three steps:

1. The position (*zenkutsu-dachi*)
2. The hip turning
3. The fist punch (*zuki*)

In this detailed analysis, we want to consider the fist punch again, and point out what constitutes a good fist punch:

1. The correct path for the punching and receding
2. The speed
3. The concentration of force (tension high point).

Review the forward stance (*zenkutsu-dachi*): The distance between both feet from the side should be 30–39 inches. The hips must be lowered as deeply as possible. (With advanced students, it may perhaps look as if they were holding their hips rather high, but at the moment of striking their legs are tensed and hips lowered.) Tense your abdominal muscles. Your navel must point slightly up.

Hip turning

Now let us practice the agile turning in of the hip, one of the most important and basic movements in Karate. The strong force of the hip must be transmitted to the arm. Without a well controlled hip movement, neither defence nor counter-attack can be effective.

Practicing the hip turning is so important for the beginner, it should be practiced continuously until it is mastered. However, in this respect, even advanced students sin a great deal. Without a good hip turn, your techniques are awkward, your movements stiff, angular, and not very forceful. Practice turning your hips again and again. It is not as simple as it looks at first.

Assume the *zenkutsu-dachi*, the forward starting stance. Rest your hands at your hips. Relax your shoulders and lower them. Tense your abdominal wall slightly. Now turn your body away 45 degrees (Illus. 47). Keep the upper part of your body erect while doing this. Now, by turning your hip back in again, you reach the starting position. At the moment your hip swings back into the starting position, all the muscles of your body must be tensed, especially the muscles of your lower body and the side muscles of your trunk (Illus. 48). The leg behind you must press forward strongly. At this point there is danger that the upper part of your body may incline forwards. To prevent this, always let your navel point slightly upwards.

Illus. 47   **Illus. 48**
Hip turning provides additional power for your gyaku-zuki punching.

Now practice the turning continuously. When you turn away, your body relaxes; when you turn back in, your body tenses. Therefore, breathe in when turning away, breathe out (tensing up) while turning back in. Practice slowly at first, then increasingly faster.

Remember that the turning originates at the hip. Turn only the hip, and your shoulders will follow by themselves. Remain erect, and always have your navel pointing slightly upwards. Press your rear leg forward strongly at the moment of turning back in.

Fist punch (zuki)

Oi-zuki

Read what has already been said about the *seiken-choku-zuki* (page 165).

Concerning the correct path of the fists, remember that your

In the two-fist punch, you start with palms up, and you reverse this as your fists spring forwards.

hands must move on a straight line that leads from your hip bone out to a point directly in front of the center of your body. Practice this with both fists and with one fist, as shown in Illus. 49, 50 and 51.

At *hachiji-dachi* (the basic position), both fists are at your hips palms up, and your elbows are pressed back (Illus. 49). Now extend both fists at the level of your solar plexus, with your thumbs touching each other slightly, and the palms of your hands pointing down (Illus. 50).

Next, draw your right fist back close to your body and turn it 180 degrees while you are doing this, so it is palm up again. Your elbow must brush the side of your body (Illus. 51). Then let your right fist come forward again. Do this exercise slowly at first, then increasingly faster. Tense your muscles when your returning fist touches your hip. Relax your muscles (inhaling) when the fist goes forward again. First practice with your right fist, then left, then both, etc.

The astonishing jolt of a Karate punch comes from several elements working together at the moment of contact. Every part of your body must be well tuned to every other part in order to make the jab effective. Speed is most important in this. Earlier we said

"Karate is speed transformed into power." The greater the speed, the greater the force.

To give the punching arm more speed, there is a little trick: The receding arm determines the speed. Therefore, draw the receding arm back as quickly and powerfully as possible. At the moment it reaches your hip, tense all your muscles sharply. (Re-read the breathing section of *seiken-choku-zuki*, page 166.) Practice a few times with right, then left.

Concentration of power

The concentrated and simultaneous working together of many muscles is more effective than the working of single muscles at different times, no matter how powerfully they work singly. It is not so simple to tense all your muscles at the proper moment. Therefore, conscious practice is necessary.

Extend both arms so that the fists touch each other slightly (Illus. 52). Now tense all your muscles, especially those of the lower part and sides of your body. Consciously, press your shoulders down towards your chest. Press the air down too and breathe out while doing this (Illus. 53). Then inhale and relax all of your muscles. Practice this.

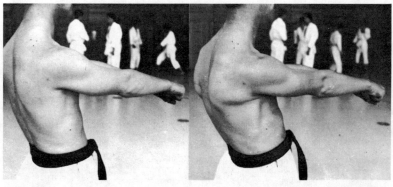

Illus. 52   **Illus. 53**
Breathing from the hara and pointing your navel slightly upwards give you extra force.

Illus. 54 (left)
Illus. 55 (right)
Practice drawing your
receding arm back rapidly to
a fist at your hip.

Exercise for the receding arm

Take the *zenkutsu-dachi* (the forward stance) turned away by 45 degrees. Your right fist is closed in the originating position on your right hip, your left hand extended to the front (Illus. 54).

Now turn your hip back in sharply and while you are doing

Illus. 56   **Illus. 57**
Practice stiffening your rear leg as your fist moves forwards in a punch.

this, draw your left hand back rapidly and powerfully on a straight line to a fist. Be sure that your elbows are pressed to your ribcage (Illus. 55). This exercise is to strengthen the sides of your body. The movements of the hip and the receding arm must be synchronized. Practice it, right and left.

Exercise for the rear leg

Take the same starting position. While you are doing this, do not hold your leg stiffly behind you, but relaxed and slightly bent (Illus. 56). Now turn your hip in again sharply, and let your fist start forward. Don't interrupt the movement when your hip reaches its forward position. Meanwhile, extend your rear leg abruptly and tense it as if you were pushing against the floor powerfully with the sole of your foot. By doing this, a counter-force results, which is transmitted through your body to the jabbing fist and increases the force of the punch (Illus. 57).

While you are doing this, check to see that your body remains erect, that you shove your hip forward and that your navel is pointing slightly upwards. Learn and feel consciously in the course of this exercise that the force of *gyaku-suki* (the reverse punch) comes out of the hip *and* out of the rear leg, and that it is transmitted to the punching fist.

The whole gyaku-zuki

Take the left *zenkutsu-dachi* (the forward stance) with your body turned away by 45 degrees. The upper part of your body must be movable, the soles of your feet pressing down on the floor, your knees elastic. Extend your left hand out straight with your elbow relaxed. Put your right fist, palm up, on your right hip, your elbow toward your backbone. Look straight ahead, drawing your chin in slightly.

As your hip is swung back in again, draw your left hand back sharply and make your fist solid while doing this. At the same time, extend your rear leg out powerfully and thrust your right fist forward on a straight line. At the moment your right arm is completely extended and your left fist drawn back to your hip, your entire body must be filled with tension and power. As for breathing, resume the starting position relaxed (breathe in). Exhale at the high tension point.

No   Yes

1. Lower your hips as deep as possible and leave the soles of your feet on the floor.

2. Move your arms so that your elbows brush along your body; in this way they will not go to the outside as you are turning your hip.

3. Try consciously not to turn your shoulders, but rather your hips, and let your shoulders follow. The thrust does not come from your shoulder, but from your hip. Relax your shoulders and try to turn your body at the hip.

4. Effective hip turning must be fast.

5. Always be sure that your navel points slightly upwards.

6. Be sure you are breathing correctly while tensing and relaxing.

The two punching techniques *oi-zuki* and *gyaku-zuki* are among the most basic techniques of Karate. For this reason, they must be practiced constantly by both beginners and masters.

Once again, here are the most important characteristics of both techniques:

Oi-zuki. The attack lands as the advancing leg sets down. This is a very fast and direct attack which receives its power from the forward propulsion of the body. For this reason, the forward movement must really be fast.

Gyaku-zuki. A very powerful punch, which gets its power from the sharp turning of the hip. The hip does not start unless the front leg is touched down. *Gyaku-zuki* is mostly used in counter-attacking.

Tate-zuki

Exactly like *seiken-choku-zuki* (the straight punch with the front of your fist), except that your extended fist makes a quarter turn,

In tate-zuki (left) the fist makes a quarter turn. In ura-zuki (right) the elbow moves in front of the body.

so that the palm is facing inwards (Illus. 58) instead of a half turn. It is applied in the same-side (*oi-zuki*) and the reverse form (*gyaku-zuki*), above all in close competition.

Ura-zuki

A technique especially used in close fighting. The fist is thrust out, starting from the hip. At the moment of contact it is turned to the outside (palm inwards) and the elbow is shoved somewhat in front of the body (Illus. 59). Tense your stomach and chest muscles above all at the moment of contact.

Mawashi-zuki

Mawashi-zuki

The fist is thrust in a half circle (roundhouse) from the hip, following an outside line unless it makes contact at right angles

The roundhouse punch from the hip (mawashi-zuki) is used most often in counter-attack.

against the temple of the opponent (Illus. 60, 61 and 62). Be sure that your fist really describes a half circle.

This is used mostly in counter-attack in the *gyaku* form in order to utilize the force of the turning in of the hip.

Kagi-zuki

The fist does not move along the body to the front center, but is punched in a hook. The elbow of the punching arm leaves the body sharply at right angles (Illus. 63).

It is used in counter-attack under the defending arm of the opponent (Illus. 64), usually from the *kiba-dachi* (straddle-leg stance).

The two hook type punches (*mawashi-zuki* and *kagi-zuki*) are not easy at first for the beginner to perform to get shock effect. Therefore, practice slowly at first, completely relaxed, and without force. Then tense all your muscles sharply at the moment of contact, especially those muscles at the side of your lower body. Practice breathing exactly as for *seiken-choku-zuki*.

Morote-zuki

Both fists start simultaneously from the hips for the same target (Illus. 65).

Illus. 63   **Illus. 64**

In kagi-zuki, swing your elbow out sharply as you strike beneath your opponent's defending arm.

Age-zuki

The starting position is at the hip as for the normal fist punch. The *age-zuki* is actually a blow rather than a punch, for the back of the fist is smashed against the chin of the opponent in an ascending arc by a snapping movement of the elbow (Illus. 66).

Illus. 65   **Illus. 66**

Morote-zuki (left) is a two-fisted punch. Age-zuki (right) is a punch with an upward swing to catch your opponent under his chin.

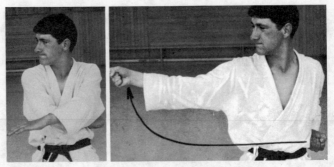

Riken-uchi is an upward side strike with the back of your fist.

3. Striking Techniques

(Uchi-waza)

In this technique, the striking is usually accomplished by a snapping motion from the elbow. The transmission of force does not occur like a thrust on a straight line, but usually from a half circle. Many striking techniques can also be used in defence.

**Illus. 69.
The fist turns at impact in riken-uchi.**

Illus. 70. In another type of riken-uchi, the back of the fist strikes downwards from the side.

Riken-uchi (also called ura-ken-uchi)

In the sidewards strike, the back of the fist is used. The fist is propelled from the elbow, crossing the body (left to right in Illus. 67 and 68). At the moment of contact, the fist turns so that the small finger side points down (Illus. 69).

In striking down, the back of the fist is again used in a wide arc with the elbow as the turning point (Illus. 67 and 70), but the fist strikes with palm up.

Riken-uchi is preferred for close fighting, as for an attack on the face or solar plexus. It can be applied to the front also from *zenkutsu-dachi*, the forward stance.

Practice both types of *riken-uchi* in this way:

Starting position: *hachiji-dachi*. Glide from this position into *kiba-dachi* (the straddle-leg) stance and strike with *riken-uchi* while doing this. The back of the fist must strike at the same moment as the leg is put down. Tension peaks in the whole body. Practice to right and left and at right angles to front and rear.

Kentui-uchi (also called tettsui-uchi)

This is exactly the same as *riken-uchi* except that the small finger side of the fist is used in striking a hammer blow.

Tettsui-uchi

Haishu-uchi

In this blow with the back of the hand, the same movement and form of practice are used as with *riken-uchi*. It is especially im-

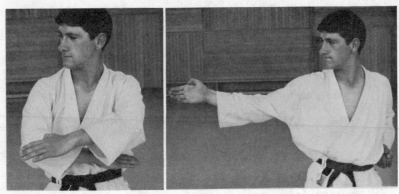

Haishu-uchi is a strike like riken-uchi but with the back of the open hand.

portant that the back of the hand be turned sharply to the outside at the time of contact (Illus. 71 and 72).

In all Karate techniques in which the open hand and the edge of the hand are used, the thumb is angled down sharply to protect it from injury (Illus. 72).

The *haishu-uchi* technique is used in attacking the diaphragm, face, temples, and ears, and above all in defence.

Open hand (nukite)

Shuto-uchi

The blow with the edge of the hand, *shuto-uchi*, is an effective and well known Karate technique. It also obtains its effect from a snapping motion from the elbow and from turning out of the wrist. There are two different types.

The first type—the blow from the outside to the inside—starts with your thumb. Bend your thumb in sharply and tense your hand (Illus. 73). Be sure that you do not raise the shoulder of your striking arm (Illus. 74). That makes it impossible to tense the side trunk muscles and chest muscles. Strike with the edge of your hand (Illus. 75).

Illus. 73   **Illus. 74**   **Illus. 75**

Shuto-uchi depends for its effectiveness on a snapping of the elbow as you swing.

Apply this strike in *zenkutsu-dachi* (the forward stance) in the same side and reverse form. In the latter, this edge-of-the-hand technique is especially effective, since the turning in of the hip acts to increase the roundhouse motion of striking.

The second type—the blow from the inside to the outside—starts with bringing the palm of your striking hand to the opposite ear (Illus. 76). Through the snapping motion of the elbow and the turning of the wrist (Illus. 77), this technique gets its effect.

Illus. 76 (left). Illus. 77 (right). Striking with the edge of your hand is shuto-uchi.

183

Illus. 78. Apply shuto-uchi at the level of your opponent's chin, and turn your body away.

At the point of contact, at the level of your opponent's chin, your body may be turned away (Illus. 78). Notice that the surface of your stretching hand faces down obliquely at the moment of contact. Techniques using the edge of the hand are equally effective when executed with the same-side form or the reverse form.

Apply *shuto-uchi* from *zenkutsu-dachi* and from *kiba-dachi*. Later, we will find it in somewhat varied form in defence (see *shuto-uke* and *gedan-uke*).

Empi-uchi backwards (ushiro-empi)

The elbow is an especially powerful and variable weapon in close fighting. Without long boring special training, you can strike with the elbow very effectively. Women can apply the elbow in self-defence especially well.

The backward blow with the elbow (*ushiro-empi*) you have already practiced many a time completely unconsciously: it is nothing more than the movement of the receding arm in the fist technique. (Pointer for trainers: the *ushiro-empi* results as a sort of by-product from the learning of the fist punch.)

In Illus. 79, your opponent has wrapped his arms around you and grabbed your upper arm from the rear. How do you get loose? You bring both your hands together in front of your chest, with the palms of your hands up. Now assume the *kiba-dachi* (straddle-leg) position to the left, and thrust your arms forward at the same

Illus. 79   **Illus. 80**   **Illus. 81**

Escape from a bear hug ending in ushiro-empi, a backwards blow with your elbow.

time. While doing this, rotate your elbows and turn your hands (still together) so that at the end your palms are facing down. In doing this, a lever effect occurs in your upper arms which breaks your opponent's embrace. By lowering your hip to the side at the same time, you will break free (Illus. 80). In the course of this entire movement, your spine must remain vertical. Start the movement from your hip (from the *hara*). Once free, you need only to rip your extended right arm down and to the rear. The *empi-uchi* (backward blow with the elbow) hits exactly in the pit of your opponent's stomach (Illus. 81).

Empi-uchi to the front (mae-empi)

Start with your left fist at your hip. Your right hand swings out to the front, relaxed (Illus. 82). Now the elbow of your right arm is thrust straight to the front towards its target as your arm tenses and your wrist turns over (Illus. 83). The targets are usually the solar plexus or the ribs. However, this blow can also be aimed against the head (Illus. 84). (See next page.)

Your body may be turned in the course of this, but remember that you should be anchored so that your navel always points up slightly. Otherwise, your shoulder can very easily come forward in this technique.

Illus. 82

Illus. 83

Illus. 84
Empi-uchi is an effective elbow strike. To the front (called mae-empi) it can be aimed at the solar plexus or ribs or at the head. See page 185.

Yoko-empi is an elbow thrust to the side.

Practice this with the same side and reverse forms, out of *zenkutsu-dachi*, the forward stance.

Empi-uchi to the side (yoko-empi)

Thrust your elbow sharply to the side and turn your wrist in doing this (Illus. 85-86). The elbow of your striking arm will hit exactly on the nipple of the opponent's chest (Illus. 86). If it were to continue, your elbow would describe a slight arc to the rear, but you would no longer be able to tense the muscles of your lower body and the muscles at the side of your torso.

The *yoko-empi* is used almost exclusively from the *kiba-dachi* (straddle-leg) position. Practice it starting from *hachiji-dachi*, the basic position. Glide to the right, to the left, at right angles, right and left forwards and backwards, into *kiba-dachi*. While doing this, complete the *yoko-empi* simultaneously each time you place your leg down. This is the same practice form as in *riken-uchi* (the sidewards strike) out of *kiba-dachi*. Always strike with your elbow, which points the direction.

Empi-uchi upwards (age-empi)

Start in position with your fist at your hip. Now swing your elbow sharply upwards (Illus. 87) and turn your fist while you are doing this, so that your palm faces your ear. The point of

Illus. 87. Age-empi is an
upward blow with the elbow.

Illus. 88

Illus. 89

your elbow will strike the opponent in front of the middle of his chin (Illus. 89). For that reason, your body must be turned away somewhat, your head inclined away.

The *age-empi* can also be struck to the front against your opponent's solar plexus (Illus. 88).

Application of *age-empi* is mostly out of *zenkutsu-dachi* (the forward position) in the reverse form (as counter-attack) or the same-side form.

Shita-empi

Illus. 90

Illus. 91

Illus. 92

Illus. 93

Empi-uchi down (shita-empi)

Illus. 90–93 show downward striking with the elbow against your opponent's chest and neck. The elbow techniques all require short, sharp action and immediate release (tension and relaxation).

Practice all elbow techniques this way: Starting position normal in *hachiji-dachi*, the basic position.

Tempo 1: *mae-empi* (to the front), sharp tensing up, immediate release, and then

Tempo 2: *yoko-empi* (to the side), then

Tempo 3: *ushiro-empi* (backwards), then

Tempo 4: *age-empi* (upwards), and

Tempo 5: *empi-uchi* down (*shita-empi*).

After short relaxation (inhaling), count again: 1, 2, 3, 4, 5, perform the actions, and go on. Finally, carry out all techniques at the same tempo. After this, practice to the left.

Here is a practice form of the fist blow in connection with *ushiro-empi*: Rip the extended arm back to *ushiro-empi* (tempo 1), then thrust your fist of the same arm forwards (tempo 2), then do both techniques at one speed. Give a short, sharp exhale at the moment of the fist blow to the front.

Once again for review:

Do you still remember that as each technique is carried out, your navel must point slightly upwards? Do you always breathe correctly in a way that helps you tense and relax alternately? In executing each technique, and each movement, do you still recall that every fast, powerful movement must originate from the hip, that the *hara* is your focus, which you must preserve, so that you do not lose your balance? Always imagine that your "middle" is just below your navel. Practice correct breathing to help you strengthen this *hara*. Only then will each one of your movements and techniques be sure and powerful, starting from your inner balance, your *hara*, surely and powerfully.

Be increasingly conscious of the fact that the strength for your fist jab, for example, does not come from the arm—as the beginner thinks—but from the *hara*. Correct breathing helps you a great deal in doing this—a portion of the air is pressed down against the abdominal wall as you exhale.

Illus. 94. Quick kick is the rule in Karate.

4. Kicking Techniques
(Keri-waza)

The use of the leg as a weapon is a unique characteristic of Karate. In daily life, your legs are not utilized in varied activities or in as many different ways as your arms. For that reason, your legs must be exercised persistently, for you to use them well as weapons. When using kicking techniques, you must pay particular attention to the supporting leg. In order to preserve your balance,

Illus. 95
Start

Illus. 96
Mae-geri-ke-age

Illus. 97
Mae-geri-ke-komi

your supporting leg must stand strongly, particularly in the direction of the thrust of your foot. In addition, it must be able to absorb the shock when your foot strikes its target. For this reason, the supporting leg must always be slightly bent and elastic at the knee. During the thrust, the entire sole of your foot must remain on the ground.

The instantaneous pulling back of your thrusting leg, which must take place as quickly as the actual thrust itself, is very important for maintaining your balance. Not only do your leg muscles work when using leg techniques, but, as is the case with every Karate technique, you must use your entire body as well, and, in this case, the power of your hip particularly.

Mae-geri, the front kick

In *mae-geri*, the ball of the foot strikes. Therefore, your toes must be sharply clenched in at an angle. There are two types of *mae-geri*:

1. *Mae-geri-ke-age*
In this kick, it is chiefly the snapping motion of the knee that is utilized. The ball of your foot thrusts upwards ("age" means "lift") and strikes your partner's chin, armpit, chest, or stomach,

like an uppercut from below. Starting from the *hachiji-dachi* (basic) position, draw up your knee as high as possible towards your chest. In doing this, keep your foot parallel to the floor, your toes angled sharply away (Illus. 95). Without interruption, now propel your foot up (Illus. 96) and spring back into the starting position with the foot at the supporting knee (Illus. 95) in a single uninterrupted movement. Note that the supporting knee and leg remain stationary. Use tempo 1 for the ripping up of the knee, the kick, and the springing back of the foot to the knee. Use tempo 2 for placing down your foot—this is a separate tempo speed.

Be sure that the toes of your supporting leg point straight ahead and that the knee and the toes of your kicking leg point straight ahead as well. Only in this way can you concentrate all of the muscles of your body into the thrust.

2. *Mae-geri-ke-komi*

In this technique, the foot is thrust straight to the target, noticeably using the hip (Illus. 97). When doing this, you can strike with the ball of your foot or your heel. Strike with your heel when practicing, angle up your toes sharply when doing it.

The *mae-geri* is usually carried out from the *zenkutsu-dachi* or forward position with one leg behind. Use the *mae-geri-ke-age* when your distance from your partner is not too great and when he is bent slightly forward. Use the *mae-geri-ke-komi* from a greater distance—it is very powerful as the hip is thrust in the direction of the target.

Mae-geri

Illus. 98   Practice   Illus. 99

Illus. 100. Ke-age   Illus. 101. Ke-komi

Follow Illus. 98–101 for practice forms of *mae-geri-ke-age* and *ke-komi*. Your partner stretches out his hand at the level of his chin. You stand in front of him in such a way that his fingertips touch your chin (Illus. 98). Now assume *zenkutsu-dachi* from the rear (Illus. 99). First kick *mae-geri-ke-age* with the ball of your foot to the palm of your partner (Illus. 100). Place your leg down again to *zenkutsu-dachi* (Illus. 99), then execute *mae-geri-ke-komi* towards his solar plexus (Illus. 101). Thrust your hip strongly in the direction of the target. With the *ke-komi*, you are a good arm's length further away from the target than with *ke-age*.

Illus. 102

Illus. 103

Practice stance for mae-geri exercises.

For further practice, stand in another basic position, *heisoku-dachi*, knees and feet together, large toes touching each other, knees slightly bent (Illus. 102 and 103).

Now do *mae-geri-ke-age* 10 times to the right, then 10 to the left, and while doing it, try to kick as high as possible. (Between each blow, set your leg down.) You will notice that even when doing *ke-age*, your hip must be shoved slightly forward. Above all, you will find that your knee must be taken as high up towards the chest as possible, and that after the kick it must return to this position. This exercise is also very good for your balance. Lifting your knee up high is very important in all leg techniques. For that reason, you need a few more exercises which force you to get your knee up as high as possible.

Knee exercises

Draw your knee up as high as possible to your chest and hold it with your hands. Remain erect while doing this and do not bend away at the hip (Illus. 104). Alternate left and right legs.

Practicing the mae-geri over an obstacle

For best results, stand behind an obstacle, such as a low bench,

Illus. 105

a tight string, belt, or similar, in the *zenkutsu-dachi* or *heisoku-dachi* position, and kick out so closely that your foot in *mae-geri* just passes over the obstacle without touching it. Your knee has to be drawn up (Illus. 105 and 106).

Now practice *mae-geri* on signal. The knee, to go past the obstacle, must be up very high towards your chest before and after the kick.

Target practice

Your partner again stands in front of you and stretches out his hand at chin level. You kick for it 10 times from *zenkutsu-dachi* with *mae-geri-ke-age*, using your right leg, then 10 times with your left leg. Now your partner holds his hand next to him at the level of his stomach so that his palm is towards you. Kick with the ball of your foot and, when kicking, throw your hip in the direction of the kick.

A little variant for advanced students: Your partner changes the position of his hand after every kick so that you have to adjust quickly to a new target.

Illus. 106

| Illus. 107 | Illus. 108 | Illus. 109 |

Yoko-geri, the side kick

In doing this, kick with the outside edge of your foot. Your foot must be positioned obliquely in such a way that the sole of your foot is as parallel as possible with the floor (Illus. 109). There are two types of *yoko-geri*:

1. *Yoko-geri-ke-age*

You must raise your knee as high as possible (Illus. 107) and sling your foot out from the knee without interruption (Illus. 108). Spring back to the knee position (Illus. 107) and place it down.

2. *Yoko-geri-ke-komi*

In this case, you start from the same position (Illus. 107), but

Yoko-geri

at the moment of striking, your hip is thrust in the direction of the goal (Illus. 109 and 110), and your foot is turned sole down as much as possible. Do not lean the upper part of your body too much in the opposite direction from the target, but push your arms in the direction of the target. In Illus. 110 you see the direct use of the hip clearly.

Illus. 111. You can practice Karate kicks out-of-doors as well as indoors.

Practice these kicks from all positions, especially from *kiba-dachi* (the straddle-leg position) in transition and in turning, but also especially out of *zenkutsu-dachi* (the forward position) with your rear leg.

Illus. 112. Gymnastic exercise to strengthen knee and leg.

Functional gymnastic exercises

Lift your knee as high as possible with the aid of your hand (Illus. 112), alternately left and right.

Practice with a partner: Stand in front of your partner in *kiba-dachi* so that you turn your side to him. Measure off the distance so that with one transition step you come into attacking distance. Now take a transition step towards your partner, who is standing in *hachiji-dachi* (the basic position), draw your leg as high up as possible, and move as if to clobber him in the chest with *yoko-geri-ke-komi*. Never use full strength, but just touch your partner. Now your partner takes your foot in both his hands and draws it higher. Make sure your supporting leg is in the correct position. Move your arms and the upper part of your body towards your partner and stay as erect as possible. When your partner releases your foot, place it down towards him in *kiba-dachi* and follow with a transition step back into the starting position. Practice

10 times to the right, then partners change and repeat, then 10 times to the left, then change and repeat.

Kicking above an obstacle

This is similar to *mae-geri* (the front kick), but don't use a bench, rather a rope or two belts tied together and held by two partners 32 inches from the floor. Take your position at the side of it in *kiba-dachi*, take your transition step, then draw your knee up high, and kick above the obstacle, put your leg back, and place it down in *kiba-dachi* facing the rope. Then back to the starting position with a transition step. If you fail to lift your knee high up to your chest before and after, you will get stuck on the obstacle.

Heisoku-dachi

Yoko-geri from heisoku-dachi

Lift your knee up rapidly, and propel your foot to the side and upwards without interrupting the movement. Note the participation of your hip, as in the case of *ke-age*. Bring your foot back to your knee and then place it down again into *heisoku-dachi* (knees and feet close together). This is a very good balance exercise. Turn the upper part of your body in the direction of the target. Try 10 kicks right, then 10 left. Be sure that when you set down your foot, your knees and your big toes are next to each other.

Finally, a somewhat more difficult exercise:

Draw your right leg up high to the side and hold it with your right hand, as in the exercise for *yoko-geri*. Now kick it sideways with *yoko-geri* (*ke-age* or *ke-komi*) and then let it spring back into your hand. Without placing your right leg down, kick 10 times, then do the same with your left leg. One purpose is to hold your balance so well that your supporting leg remains in the same spot throughout the powerful kicks. Do not bend your hip. Remain erect with the upper part of your body, and look in the direction of your target.

Illus. 113

Illus. 114

**Practice kicking ke-komi and
ke-age with a partner.**

Illus. 115

Practice with a partner

Take your partner by the sleeve. Lift your knee (Illus. 113) and
kick first with *ke-komi* towards his upper thigh (Illus. 114), then
draw your leg back and put it down. Then kick with *ke-age*
towards his armpit (Illus. 115). You first lift up your knee quickly
and then propel your foot towards the target without interruption.
Now it's your partner's turn to kick. Keep changing sides.

Target practice

Practice kicking towards the hand of your partner as in *mae-
geri*. In addition to practice of the *ke-age* alone, there is another
exercise: Tie a belt at the level of your chest around a projection.
Hold the end in one hand and then strike the belt with a *ke-age*
kick from below. Pay attention to correct position of your feet.

Illus. 116   Illus. 117

Ushiro-geri, kick to the rear

In this kick, you strike with your heel. You again draw up your knee, and then thrust your foot directly to the rear (Illus. 116 and 117). Upper thighs should keep contact with each other as long as possible, and your leg must be extended as completely as possible (Illus. 118).

Illus. 118.
Ushiro-geri.

Ushiro-geri, the backwards kick.

Rapid withdrawal of your leg is also especially important in this kick in order not to lose your balance. Bend the upper part of your body, but not too far away, and rather attempt to launch it in the direction of your target.

Stretching exercises for ushiro-geri

Stand in the *heisoku-dachi* position (knees and feet together) in front of your partner again and turn your back to him. Then take bearings over your shoulder and strike at his solar plexus with *ushiro-geri* (not too forcefully). When you do this, you should just touch his chest (Illus. 119). Your partner then grabs your foot with both hands and lifts it up. Pay attention to the correct position of your foot (heel up) and to your supporting leg. The upper part of your body should be in the direction of the target.

Another form of exercise: First kick forward with *mae-geri* and then, quickly and powerfully, without placing your foot down, kick to the rear with *ushiro-geri* (Illus. 120). Then you can also add a *yoko-geri* as well, without placing your foot down. Balance! Do this exercise several times in succession without touching down the leg that is doing the striking. But make each single kick of your foot powerful and exact.

Illus. 121   Illus. 122   Illus. 123

Three steps in performing mawashi-geri.

Mawashi-geri, the roundhouse kick

In doing this kick, you utilize the snapping movement of your knee and the turning movement of your hip in order to attack your opponent from the side with the ball or rear of your foot.

Lift up your leg, keeping it horizontal to the floor (Illus. 121) and then propel it rapidly forwards without interruption (Illus. 122). While you are doing this, turn your body along with the motion so that your supporting leg is turned 45 degrees to the side

Mawashi-geri

(90 degrees at the most). Strike sharply and snap your knee back quickly, then assume the starting position again with your supporting leg turning back in (Illus. 123). Try in this case to hold the upper part of your body as straight as possible.

Exercises for mawashi-geri

Starting from the *hachiji-dachi* (basic) position, lift up your right leg horizontally and to the side (Illus. 124), using both hands (right hand on your ankle, left hand on your knee). Do this alternately with your right leg and then your left. When you do this, your knee must point slightly upwards. Keep the inner edges of your other foot on the floor.

One more exercise on the floor: Sit with both your legs stretched out in front of you. Then bend back your right leg so that the entire inner surface of the leg touches the floor. (This is the same position the leg will take—but in the air—in *mawashi-geri*.) Then rock forward twice with outstretched arms so that your forehead touches your knee. Then turn the upper part of your body to the rear with outstretched arms, and rock twice to the rear, twice to the front again, and so on.

Stretching exercise with a partner: Stand in the left *zenkutsu* (forward) position, your partner too. Then thrust with *mawashi-geri* so that your foot strikes past his neck. (Do not put any force into the kick.) Your partner catches your leg (Illus. 125) and straightens it up more and more. It is all right if it "pulls." Pay attention to the correct position of your supporting leg (do not turn it too far to the side). Extend your attacking leg and hold the upper part of your body straight. Let it loose—put it down. Now it's your partner's turn. Following this, practice the exercise to the left as well.

Now a somewhat more difficult exercise: Starting from the position of the first exercise (drawing up your leg with your hands) strike with a *mawashi-geri*, let your knee spring back, catch it with your hands and kick again without putting it down. Do this 10 times. When this exercise is working well and your supporting leg remains on the same spot while you are kicking, you have achieved good balance. In addition, practice this from the *heisoku-dachi*

Illus. 124

Exercises for mawashi-geri.

position (knees and feet together), kick at a right angle to the direction of your foot, and turn back again to the *heisoku-dachi* position.

Some more types of exercise: Advance in the *zenkutsu-dachi* (forward) position with *mawashi-geri*. Advance in the *kokutsu-dachi* (back stance) position with *mawashi-geri*.

A form of exercise with a partner: Stand in the *zenkutsu-dachi* position to the left. Your partner should stand opposite you in the *zenkutsu-dachi* position to the right; his shoulders should be turned away at a 45-degree angle. Now you can strike your partner's chest at exactly a right angle from the side using *mawashi-geri* from the right. Now your partner should take one step backwards as you put down the leg with which you were kicking. You can now kick his chest again immediately, using *mawashi-geri* from the left. Advance continuously with *mawashi-geri* from the right and from the left. When you reach the end of the available space, return to where you started. Now let your partner take his turn. When you are doing this exercise always have a target in mind. That develops the feeling for distance which you absolutely

207

have to have when practicing Karate. In addition, you have to adapt yourself to your partner's movements, something which must also be developed in actual Karate.

Kansetsu-geri

Fumi-komi, the stamping kick (also called kansetsu-geri)

This is a downward-directed kick which you can use forwards, sidewards, or to the rear against the shin, the bridge of the foot, or the back of the knee. It can also be used against an opponent who is on the ground. You strike with your heel or with the outside edge of your foot. This blow is not basically different from the other foot techniques except that it must be "stamped" downwards in a *ke-komi* manner.

Hiza-geri, the kick with the knee

Like the elbow, the knee is a very powerful weapon in close fighting. The knee technique can be a by-product in the course of *mae-geri*. It is nothing more than lifting your knee sharply

Illus. 126. Hiza-geri, the knee kick used in close fighting.

against your partner's chest before you actually perform the kick with your foot. (Illus. 126). Use it in self-defence in the course of being grasped by your opponent's hands, or being choked, or when you are being grabbed at the shoulders, etc.

In concluding, we must examine two more kicking techniques called Tobi in Japanese, which have a sensational effect—this is the reason you frequently see them in photos. These are attacks with your foot from the air and from jumping.

Illus. 127. The advancing foot attack from the air—called mae-tobi-geri.

Mae-tobi-geri or ni-dan-geri

In this advancing foot attack from the air, you can kick once, twice, or three times (Illus. 127). If you find you are merely kicking the air with your foot attack, then step to your left, for example, and kick to the right. This is not an especially difficult kick to learn. However, to deceive your opponent with your first attack, start by kicking towards his chest, or strike his cover (defence) out of the way and follow this up with a second attack. Then it becomes more significant.

Practice in this way: If you are kicking with your right leg, advance a step to the right and then *mae-geri* to the left without interruption. Immediately after doing this, spring sideways to the right and do *mae-geri* into the air. Practice for a while in this

Illus. 128. Yoko-tobi-geri is generally considered a beautiful attack.

manner. Then increase the power you put into your jump to the side. Take a short run, jump to the side, then first kick into the air to the left, and finally make your actual attack against the opponent's face to your right. You will notice that you will no longer have difficulty in kicking twice with your foot in the air after this preliminary exercise.

If possible, practice this attack with a tall sandbag. Spring up from a low position with at most a run of one step. Also try to jump up from a very deep position with the aid of the tension in your legs without a running start. (If the leg with which you are kicking is your right leg, then your right leg is in front.)

Yoko-tobi-geri

This is a very beautiful attack. It starts from a jump and there are a few difficulties learning how to perform it. Nevertheless, a good Karateka should take the trouble to learn it.

The *yoko-tobi-geri*, actually an attack to the side with your foot in the air, requires you to jump past your opponent and then kick to the side. The greatest difficulty is that the leg from which you jump must be slapped up against the attacking leg as you finish the attack with your foot (Illus. 128).

Now start the exercise as follows: with the left leg the jumping leg, first jump up and down several times in one spot with both legs. Continue, but after every second hop, slap the foot of your supporting leg (the right) to the knee of your jumping leg (the left). Every other time, make a hop without slapping your springing leg. Hop this way for some time. Doing this, slapping the foot of your supporting leg to your jumping leg, will become so automatic that in a short time you will be doing it like a reflex.

As the next step, take a running start, spring up quickly, and kick to the side with your attacking leg. (You do not need to jump high at all.) Probably you will discover for yourself the next difficulty: Your arms will be floating around in the air. You will succeed that much better in bringing your arms down, the more intensively you have practiced the preliminary exercise of slapping the foot of your supporting leg on your springing leg. You can concentrate on your arms much more easily if you no longer have to pay conscious attention to your legs.

The next step then is to practice the actual *yoko-tobi-geri* with a sandbag. Illus. 129 shows *yoko-tobi-geri* in a match.

Illus. 129. Yoko-tobi-geri in a match.

Exercises for foot techniques

Here is an exercise you can do at home (you need only a few minutes) or as a setting-up exercise preceding a practice session. It is useful for all foot techniques because it especially develops the power for the snapping movement of your knee.

1. As a daily exercise, lift your right thigh parallel to the ground from the *hachiji-dachi* (basic) position. Let your foot snap forwards quickly 10 times. Do the same exercise with your left leg. Then lift your right thigh up to the side and snap your foot to the side 10 times. Then the left leg. Pay attention to the correct position of your feet. You will notice the increase in power in your foot techniques very quickly, and you will also find this exercise naturally good training for balance.

The feet are very powerful weapons with a wide range. However, in order to be able to use them effectively, you must practice leg techniques continuously in many forms.

2. An indispensable aid for developing exactness is target practice. You must be able to strike right in the bull's-eye with your feet. Here are a few more ideas for target practice to train your eye: Suspend a small ball (for example, a tennis ball on a string) at chest level. Kick at it with all your strength so that your kick stops in front of it or only touches it lightly. First kick 10 times to the right with *mae-geri-ke-age*, and then to the left. After doing this, practice the same thing with *yoko-geri-ke-age* and then with *mawashi-geri*. Then, after some time, hang the ball up somewhat higher—at a maximum, at chin height. Be sure when doing the *mae-geri* that you touch the ball lightly with the BALL of your foot. You will develop a very good eye after some time with this exercise. You can also use a partner as a target. He should take the *kiba-dachi* (straddle-leg position) in front of you. Aim for his chin in the same manner.

3. A very advantageous exercise for foot techniques is a combination of kicks. Here is an excellent combination which you should practice in every training session: Advance with *mae-geri* (front kick) to the right and to the left, then with *yoko-geri* (side kick) to the right and to the left, then with *ushiro-geri* (kick to the rear) to the right starting from the turning of your body, and then

Kansetsu-geri   **Ushiro-geri**

mae-geri once again to the left. Thus, you will advance continuously in the same direction always alternating your right and left legs. Pay attention first to drawing your knee up high in every technique. As you advance with the foot techniques, throw your body (the *hara*) forwards.

4. Your partner stands before you. Your task is to drive him off by advancing so quickly and taking up so much space that your partner can hardly keep up with you as he goes backwards. This exercise has the additional advantage for you of always keeping a target for your foot techniques before your eyes so that you do not merely have to kick into empty air. Covering a great deal of ground while advancing with foot techniques is naturally an especially great advantage in a fight.

Further combinations which you can practice: Advance with *yoko-geri* to the left and then do *mawashi-geri* (roundhouse kick) to the right without a pause. In this case, you can throw your body into the second technique very nicely. *Mae-geri* and *yoko-geri* is a further combination, or the reverse, *yoko-geri* and *mae-geri*.

The most important thing for all leg techniques is lifting your knee swiftly and powerfully. The decisive thing here is whether you come up high enough with your knee technique and whether your kick is swift and powerful. Practice all techniques starting from the *heisoku-dachi* position (knees and feet together), first snapping up your knee while you are doing this, and then letting your foot snap out high without interruption.

5. There is another nice exercise which develops strength for pulling up your knee: Lean against a wall with your arms extended. Your body should be at approximately a 45-degree angle to the wall. Now lift your knees alternately to your chest.

Something more about the use of the kicks: Kicking with your feet is most effective at stomach level and lower. High kicks can be warded off more easily and put you in danger. For that reason, use high kicks only when you can execute them quickly, precisely and right in the bull's-eye.

"Stopping short" as you did with the arm technique is also valid for the leg technique. Foot techniques must also be stopped with millimeter accuracy. What helps you here is the tension in your lower body (*hara*), which makes the technique highly effective.

In order to give your foot technique the power that originates from the *hara*, your hip must not be bent in at the moment of stopping, and the upper part of your body should not be bent away. These bends prevent you from being able to tense your lower stomach. Keep in mind that if a foot technique is to be effective, your attacking foot must be invisible from your opponent from the moment it leaves the ground. Your foot must be rushed to its target with a whipping motion and then sprung back again.

5. Defense Techniques
(Uke-waza)

This chapter should actually precede the chapter on techniques for attacking. The fact of the matter is that the most important thing in true Karate is defence. This also means that the use of Karate for purposes of attack is not part of the real essence of Karate. However, the presentation of defence has been delayed on purpose, for you can understand the defences better if you know what types of attacks there are.

In Karate, the techniques of defence have a shock effect like the attacks. For this reason, by using a good defence you can rob your opponent of any further desire to attack.

First, here are some basic considerations about defence technique: By defence, we mean every activity which is suited to making an opponent's attack ineffective. The entire activity of defence must result in the opponent desisting from further attacks, or becoming incapable of any further attack because of an immediate counter-attack. Now, if you consider the problem you will find that there are four types of defences:

1. Good defensive techniques cause such great pain that the opponent loses his eagerness to continue attacking.

2. Good defensive techniques lead to a subsequent counter-attack.

3. Without defending yourself directly, you avoid the opponent's attack by turning your body swiftly and make a Karate attack yourself at the same time.

4. You make a Karate attack before your opponent attacks—in other words, you beat your opponent to the draw.

In this chapter, only the purely defensive techniques will be covered. Complete defensive actions will wait until later.

Basic principles

Every defence receives its decisive force by turning away your hips and, by doing this, the upper part of your body. Be conscious of turning with your hip and see that the upper part of your body is carried along. (See also remarks about *gyaku-zuki* — page 170 —in the section on "turning the hip.") It is not your shoulders which turn, but your hip—sharply and forcefully—carrying along the upper part of your body. Turning your body away in the course of defence has two decisive advantages: In doing this you offer your opponent very little surface to attack. Since your body is turned approximately 45 degrees to the side, you are already standing in a position ready to counter-attack in the *gyaku* form. For this reason, your counter-attack can take place swiftly and forcefully without losing any time.

The basic principle in defence for the beginner is that it be undertaken from the same side: For example, if your left leg is forward, then you must defend to the left, etc. It is only in these circumstances that the two advantages mentioned become valid.

You learned in the case of *oi-zuki* (the lunge punch) that the technique performed from the same side is the more direct and more rapid. Now, when you are defending yourself, you must be equally direct and quick. Your defence must be triggered off at the same moment as you put down your leg. Immediately thereafter you can turn in your hip sharply, and from the turned-away position of your body, begin the counter-attack. (The advanced student must also be able to defend in the *gyaku* form.)

Keep in mind that this powerful turning back and forth of your hip must be clearly visible. Later on are exercises especially tailored for this turning of your hip. However, pay attention to it consciously even now.

Since attacks are possible on the face and neck, on the upper part of the body above the belt, and on parts of the body below the belt, we correspondingly distinguish three levels of attack:

jodan—higher level
chudan—middle level
gedan—lower level

There are specific defences against attacks on each of the levels. We will begin with a defence directed at attacks on the lower level, attacks with the feet.

Lower Level Defense (gedan)

Illus. 130

Illus. 131

In gedan-barai, a backwards step and a sharp lowering of an arm act as a basic defence on the lower level.

Gedan-barai or gedan-uke

The attacking limbs are struck aside by a sharp downward blow of your lower arm. As far as the motion is concerned, the *gedan-barai* is exactly like the *shuto-uchi* from the inside to the outside (reread description on page 183), except that the movement of the arm giving the blow is downwards and that the hand is closed to a fist.

In principle, the defences of *gedan-barai* can be applied out of any position. However, practice every time in the *zenkutsu-dachi* (forward) position. Starting from the position of *hachiji-dachi* with your right arm up high (Illus. 130), step back with your left foot, reach out and strike downwards simultaneously (Illus. 131). When doing this, your wrist will turn to the outside. The defence comes to a stop at the moment your rear leg is placed downward. In the course of this, turn your hip away sharply. The fist of your defending arm will be in a position approximately 10 inches above your knee (Illus. 131). The defending is done with the external edge of your lower arm approximately two inches above your wrist.

Gedan-shuto-uke, see *shuto-uke* (page 221).

Illus. 132   **Illus. 133**
Juji-uke is a defence used mainly against front kicks. Crossed fists interposed cause the attack to be blocked.

Juji-uke or downward X-block

This defence is used particularly against kicks. To be sure, the kick must be caught in its first stage. For this reason, the defence is usually used against a kick to the front in *zenkutsu-dachi* position. When doing this, hold the upper part of your body straight. Your fists start from your right hip (or from both hips). If you are right-handed, your right fist will be above your left one (Illus. 132). Step forward in the *zenkutsu-dachi* position with your right or left foot (Illus. 133). Your fists remain vertical.

Middle Level Defense (chudan)

Illus. 134   Illus. 135

In soto-uke defence, you start your fist behind your ear, and propel it forwards
until it is in front of your opponent's chest.

Soto-uke (use of outer edge of forearm)

This is a defence using the outer (*soto*) edge of the lower arm.
As far as the movements are concerned, this technique is the same
as *shuto-uchi* (see page 182), except that your hand is closed in a
fist. Your fist starts behind your right ear (Illus. 134) and comes
to a stop in front of your opponent's chest. Turn your wrist completely so that the back of your hand faces downward. Turn your
body from the hip (Illus. 135). The elbow of the arm used for
hitting should be above the middle of the thigh of the leg which
you have forward. This is used principally from the *zenkutsu-dachi*
and the *kiba-dachi* (forward and straddle-leg) positions.

Illus. 136 shows a defence with *soto-ude-uke*. In this case, the
fist is turned downwards, but the outer edge of the arm is used.
(See next page.)

Illus. 136. Soto-ude-uke is a defence in which the outer edge of your forearm is used.

Illus. 137   Illus. 138

The uchi-uke defence is difficult to learn.

Uchi-uke

This is the defence with the inner (*uchi*) edge of the lower arm. Your fist swings from below upwards with your elbow as a turning point. It comes to a stop opposite the shoulder on the same side. When you start, the palm of your hand faces down at the left hip (Illus. 137). In the final position, the palm of your hand faces up (Illus. 138). Pay attention to this, as you need to have your elbow in position in front of your body and not to the side. It is somewhat difficult for the beginner to introduce a shock effect into this technique. Later in the book, suitable exercises will be given for all the defence techniques.

Illus. 139   **Illus. 140**

One shuto-uke defence with the edge of the hand.

Shuto-uke

This is the defence with the edge of your hand. It is very fast and can be used in many situations, but is used principally from the *kokutsu-dachi* (back stance) position.

As far as the movements are concerned, this is just like *shuto-uchi* from the inside to the outside (reread section on page 183) and also like *gedan-uke* (the lower level defence).

Illus. 141   **Illus. 142**

In shuto-uke, one hand remains in front of your chest.

Differences: (1) The angle of the arm doing the hitting (Illus. 139 and 141), and (2) the returning hand remains like a plate before your chest (Illus. 140 and 142).

At the beginning, it is very difficult to get shock effect into the arm doing the hitting, while still stopping the arm at the correct angle. Be sure the edge of your hand is straight with your wrist (Illus. 140 and 142), and is the straight continuation of your lower arm.

Shuto-uke can also be used as a defence against attacks on your face (*jodan-shuto-uke*). In this case, you defend as in *age-uke* (see page 227), except that the edge of your open hand strikes the attacking arm in an upward direction.

There is also a defence using the edge of your hand in a downward blow (*gedan-shuto-uke*). It is exactly like *gedan-barai*, only using an open hand.

Shuto-uke defence at the chudan (middle) level.

Always plan to strike with the edge of your hand in a straight line at the attacking limbs rather than in an arc. Or expressed differently: strike the attacking arm with the edge of your hand in a straight oblique line. Do not turn your wrists until the last moment, but turn your body sharply to the side while striking. Now, if you watch your tension and your breathing at the moment of striking, your defence will soon have the necessary shock effect.

Exercises with a partner

You both stand in the *hachiji-dachi* (basic) position, and your partner extends his fist to your solar plexus. Stand so close that his fist touches your chest (Illus. 143). Now glide away towards the inside at an angle of 45 degrees. While doing this, defend yourself with your left arm (Illus. 144). Hit his arm obliquely with the

| Illus. 143 | Exercise | Illus. 144 |

223

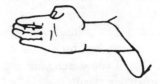

Illus. 145. An exercise to perfect your edge-of-the-hand defences.

edge of your hand. The tips of your fingers must be directly above the tip of your forward foot.

Now assume your starting position again (Illus. 143). Then slide away to the outside and defend yourself to the right (Illus. 145). Your posture must be erect in the *kokutsu-dachi* (backwards) position in the defence with *shuto-uke*. In this position, your navel must point slightly upwards so that you can put force into your technique (by breathing) and keep your balance well.

Illus. 146. Nagashi-uke sweeps the attack away with an outside-inside motion.

Nagashi-uke or sweeping barrier (jodan and chudan)

This is a very good, rapid defence which requires little strength. The attacking arm is struck away from the outside to the inside with the surface of your hand (Illus. 146). When this is done, the defence can be directed against the outside or the inside of the attacking arm. It is suitable also as a defence against attacks on the face (*jodan-tsuki*).

Upper Level Defense (jodan)

Illus. 147. The rising X-block of juji-uke at the jodan level.

Juji-uke or upward or rising X-block

You learned this defence before in the downward direction. In the same way, you can also use it upwards or rising. When using it, keep your hands open. Lay your right hand over your left hand (Illus. 147). This defence requires relatively little strength. However, it is effective only when your elbows do not peek out on both sides of your body. (Reread section on body tension, page 143.) A further advantage of this technique is that you can immediately grab with one or the other (or even both) hands and throw your opponent out of balance.

Illus. 148
Age-uke with fist.

Illus. 149
Age-uke with open hand.

Illus. 150. The Kareteka on the right is using age-uke with his fist to defend a blow at the jodan level.

Age-uke

Age-uke

Age-uke is the most commonly used defence for upper level attacks. The attacking arm is struck away in an upward direction, either with the fist (Illus. 148) or the open hand (Illus. 149). There is the characteristic twist of your wrist in this defence. In this, too, you use the outside bony edge of your lower arm (Illus. 150). When you come to a stop, your lower arm must be in front of your forehead. Turn your body to the side as you stop the blow. Do not allow your elbows to extend beyond the sides of your body. For this defence, your elbow must also be in a position directly above the middle of the thigh of your forward leg.

While this concludes the area of pure technique and its description, there are exercises you need to know for the defences and, following that, for the whole area of Karate technique.

For defending and counter-attacking:

You already know that turning your hip is the decisive factor in defending and counter-attacking. In the course of defending, your body is turned away; when you counter-attack turn it inward again. You must learn to turn your hip away and back again forcefully and obviously.

Types of exercise:

1. Continuous advancing in the *zenkutsu-dachi* (forward) position with a defence.

2. Continuous retreat in the *zenkutsu-dachi* position with a defence.

3. Continuous advancing in the *zenkutsu-dachi* position with a defence and an immediate counter-attack (*gyaku-zuki*).

4. Continuous retreat in the *zenkutsu-dachi* position with a defence and an immediate counter-attack (*gyaku-zuki*).

5. From *hachiji-dachi* (the basic position), retreat to the right in the *zenkutsu-dachi* position while defending to the left at the same time—then back to starting position. Then retreat to the left and defend to the right—and back to starting position. Now forward to the right and defend to the left. Then back and to the left.

6. The same thing, but with *gyaku-zuki* (the reverse punch) immediately following the defence. That is, always take one step backwards (right, left) and then forward. Always start from the *hachiji-dachi* position.

Advanced students can also practice the defences from the *kokutsu-dachi* (back stance) position, then turn inward to the *zenkutsu-dachi* position with *gyaku-suki*.

7. An exercise especially for the development of a hip turn: From *kiba-dachi* (straddle-leg stance), defend outwards to the front, with one arm defend with *gedan-uke* (turn the upper part of your body away with motion originating from the hip) and then counter-attack immediately with *gyaku-zuki*. Now defend with your other arm. Then with *soto-uke*, *uchi-uke*, *age-uke*. Always more to the right and to the left with an immediate counter-attack. This exercise is particularly valuable. It forces you to pay attention to turning your hips completely and consciously and develops the elasticity in your knees which you will need for every good Karate technique. This form of practice also requires little space and can be done very well at home. At the same time, if you leave out the foot movements, you can concentrate completely on turning your hips.

For defending with *shuto-uke* in connection with a counter-attack, usually the following forms are used:

Shuto-uke (edge-of-the-hand defence) in *kokutsu-dachi* (back stance). Place your leading leg the width of your shoulders to the side and rest on the ball of your foot into the *zenkutsu-dachi* (forward) position, then assume this position quickly. Immediately, counter-attack with *gyaku-zuki* (the reverse punch). The weight of your body, which is on your rear leg in the *kokutsu-dachi* position, is thrown forward by energetically straightening your bent rear leg. Thereby your counter-attack is intensified.

There is another very nice form of practice which develops hip turning in defence and counter-attack, and helps you to carry out the defences with a reflex action:

Both partners stand approximately a yard apart in the *hachiji-dachi* (basic) position. Then one partner strikes towards the face of his opponent with his fist, stopping short of course. The second partner defends with *age-uke* (rising blow at upper level), and then he strikes towards the face of his partner, who now also defends with *age-uke*.

Now the first partner strikes at the middle level and the defence is made with *soto-uke* (outer edge of lower arm). Then the second partner takes his turn, and finally the same thing is done with the lower level, where the defence used is *gedan-barai* (downward blow of lower arm).

Now you start over again from the beginning, doing the exercise continuously for some time. After a while, the execution of the defences will become more and more automatic and unconscious, a goal that is to be aimed at in the entire technique of Karate.

A coach can incorporate this exercise into regular gymnastics to great advantage.

Elasticity in your knees

When we considered *gyaku-zuki* (the reverse punch) in detail (page 170), we found that the rear leg must be elastic, that it should be relaxed and slightly bent, and that it is not tensed suddenly until the attack is made. This elasticity in your knees has a particular significance in connection with defending and counter-attacking. To be sure, the beginner is always taught that the position must always be correct, i.e., in the case of *zenkutsu-dachi* (forward position) that the rear leg must always be extended. How-

Illus. 151. The kiba-dachi position after defending with soto-uke. See the next page for your next move.

ever, the advanced student must be able to relax somewhat from this strict form in order to arrive at a mobile, effective technique. He must penetrate somewhat more deeply and understandingly into the matter.

In the case of *gyaku-zuki*, you soon learn that the force comes from your hips and your rear leg. Now, in connection with defending, the rear leg may bend somewhat when you turn your hips in the *zenkutsu-dachi* position. In the subsequent counter-attack, extend your leg energetically again and intensify its strength by doing this. (Reread under *gyaku-zuki* the exercise for the rear leg, page 175).

In other cases too, the advanced student must have elastic knees to make a technique most effective. For example, stand in the *kiba-dachi* position (Illus. 151). Perhaps you have escaped your opponent's attack this way or you have just defended with *soto-uke* from the inside.

If you want, for example, to attack with *yoko-empi-uchi* (elbow thrust to the side), you can only utilize the strength from your arm. (The *yoko-empi*, as you learned it, receives its force chiefly from the sideward advance of your body in the *kiba-dachi* position.) Since in this case you are already standing in the *kiba-dachi* position, the strength from your arm by itself will not make the *yoko-empi* very effective. Nevertheless, you know that the entire body should always participate in a good Karate technique. So, pull

Illus. 152

Illus. 153

Counter-attacking with drawn-back fist. Shift your center of gravity forward even though your feet don't change position.

back your fist and bend your entire body from the knees up. Then you strike out elastically. In this action, the center of gravity of your body is first displaced somewhat to your rear leg elastically by means of your knee (Illus. 151). Then you pull yourself together and throw your body forward again into the clean *kiba-dachi* position simultaneously with your attack (Illus. 152 and 153). By doing this you get your entire body behind the attack. When your attack reaches its goal, you have again assumed the *kiba-dachi* position. In other words, in the course of defending, you shift your weight (very elastically) to your rear leg (somewhat similar to the *kokutsu-dachi* or back position) and then throw it forward again elastically as you counter-attack going into the correct *kiba-dachi* position. This principle is also valid for *riken-uchi* (strike with the back of the fist), *tettsui-uchi* (side of the fist), and *haishu-uchi* (back of the hand) from the *kiba-dachi* position.

Practice this way: Stand in the *kiba-dachi* position and then reach out with *yoko-empi* to the left as you simultaneously shift your center of gravity slightly and elastically to your right leg. Then throw your body's center of gravity to the left again so that it is distributed on both legs at the same time as you use your technique for attacking your goal. Do the same thing to the right. Then perform *riken-uchi*, and so forth. This exercise develops elasticity in your knees, something which you must have if your Karate technique is to be good.

The speed and force of the techniques

Speed and force are always interrelated in a good Karate technique. You already know that Karate is nothing but speed transformed into force. However, swift motions are possible only when you are relaxed. Force alone (particularly powerful muscles, which precede force) cannot do it either. For Karate you need something that combines the two—speed and force.

In section on body tension (page 143), you read that the person who masters his body tension is also master of relaxing his body. As far as Karate is concerned, you actually need both. Relaxation is important for the quick supple movements; the utmost tension is needed at the moment of striking.

The fibres of your muscles change their state of tension and contract simultaneously with every step you take and with every bend of your arms. Movements are possible because of this contraction of your muscles; this natural form of muscle movement is called "isotonic." If your limbs encounter resistance that prevents movement, then the fibres of your muscles do not contract in spite of great tension of your muscles. This form of muscle work without contraction at the same time is called "isometric," in the technical language of medicine.

During the 1920's, two scientists discovered that isometric tension of a muscle can strengthen it. They tied down one leg of a frog, but allowed him to move his other leg freely. The frog kept moving his free leg and struggling incessantly in the hope of getting himself free. After some time, the researchers observed that the muscles in the leg which had been fastened down were stronger than in the leg which had been trained by continuous motion. At that time, they were not able to explain this astonishing observation. Not until 1953 could the phenomenon be explained, after great progress had been made in the study of physiology of muscles, thanks to preliminary work of two Nobel prize winners, Otto Meyerhof and Archibald Vivian Hill. Not all muscle fibres in a bundle are called into play in the course of movements. Since most movements, such as those involved in physical work, are continuously repeated, the human body accustoms itself to using only part of the muscle fibres. In general, only about 60 per cent of the fibres are involved in working. It is different in the case of isometric tension. If resistance prevents the contraction of a muscle, then all its fibres are taxed. It has been determined that continuous contractions of the muscle fibres do not provide the stimulus for strengthening the musculature and the building of new fibres, but that tension alone is responsible for this.

Several years passed after 1953 until further details of muscle growth were clarified. Muscles develop best of all when they are tensed regularly, but only for the duration of a few seconds every time. A stimulus which lasts longer than 8 seconds does not encourage muscle growth. About 1960, the first exact instructions were worked out by muscle physiologists and sports physicians for isometric training according to a plan. It is interesting to note that I have found isometric exercises by the Japanese in an old English book on Jiu-jitsu. In addition, I found in a book about Okinawa Karate nothing other than the isometric exercises which science has discovered so recently.

There are a great many isometric exercises. Everyone can invent some by using his own imagination.

The only exercises of interest here are those which represent a particular advantage for Karate. The tension in Karate exists only for a short moment and at that point as many muscle fibres as possible should be tensed. Therefore, the isometrics should be chosen in such a way that exactly those groups of muscles are trained which are needed at the moment of striking.

This is exactly what our isometric exercises are aimed at. We exert resistance from the direction and counter-pressure in the direction that takes place in Karate movements. Some exercises for defence are illustrated as follows:

Isometric exercises to strengthen your arms.

Illus. 154—for *gedan-uke* (downward blow of lower arm).
Illus. 155—for *soto-ude-uke* (outer edge of lower arm, fist down).
Illus. 156—for *age-uke* (upward arm thrust).
Illus. 157—for *uchi-ude-uke* (inner edge of lower arm, fist down).
Illus. 158—for *shuto-uke* (edge of hand).

Illus. 159

Illus. 160

Practice in the *kiba-dachi* position, inhale, grab, and then exhale while exerting strong counter-pressure, and count to seven.

Exercises for attacking:

Illus. 159—for *kagi-zuki* (hook jab).

Illus. 160—for the blow with your fist.

Even more examples can be found with a little imagination, but those which are illustrated are sufficient.

Pointers:

If these exercises—which really do not take much time—are practiced regularly before every training session or at home, then you will very quickly notice a significant increase of force at the moment of striking. Also, you will develop great agility and speed in carrying out the individual techniques as a complementary effect of the exercise for tension.

For strengthening in general, you can invent a great many isometric exercises yourself. For example, press the palm of your hand against your forehead while exerting strong pressure in the opposite direction; press your palms against each other; press your linked hands against the back of your neck, and so on.

Illus. 161   Illus. 162   Illus. 163

Exercise borrowed from a Chinese master of Karate.

Here are a few strengthening exercises, especially valuable for Karate and Judo, which come from a Chinese master of Karate. They can be done very well with a belt, although originally practiced with a thick rope.

1. Grasp the belt as in Illus. 161. Go to the other side slowly after having tensed to your utmost while inhaling. Return while exhaling. This is one cycle. Practice it 6 times.

2. Illus. 162 and 163: Grasp and pull to the outside with both hands, inhale, and move your arms slowly downward. Then return upward again while exhaling. Practice 6 times.

Illus. 164   Illus. 165

3. Illus. 164 and 165: Put your foot into the belt loop and hold the ends with your extended hand. Inhale and draw it upward slowly against the counter-pressure of your foot. Exhale and return downwards slowly. Once again this forms a complete cycle. Practice 6 times.

These exercises can also be practiced while you are lying on the floor. Lie on your back when doing this. In the case of exercises 1 and 2, lift your extended legs approximately 4 inches from the floor (training for your stomach muscles). Lift the back of your neck while doing this. Continue to breathe in the same way in this position (breathe from the diaphragm). Exercise 1 can also be done while you lie on your stomach.

If all these exercises are carried out just once with great tension and counter-pressure, even a person who is athletically trained will have sore muscles the following day.

The exercises should not be practiced more than 6 times a day. The increase in your strength will be truly astonishing after you have practiced regularly for a short time. Judoka can also profit a great deal from these exercises.

Another good method to attain speed and force in attacking and defending is training with dumbbells. Use the small dumbbells weighing 1 to 3 pounds, which you can take in one hand.

To practice the blow with your fist:

1. Take a dumbbell in your right hand. Assume the starting position with your right hip. Your left hand, which is moving to the rear, is free. If you concentrate completely on the fact that your left hand moving to the rear determines your speed, and you move your hands back and forth quickly and forcefully, then the blow with your fist will also be quick and forceful. Do this exercise 10 times with the dumbbell in your right hand, then 10 times without the dumbbell. Then practice with the dumbbell in your left hand.

Hold dumbbells in both of your hands. Strike with alternate hands. Then strike a few times without the dumbbells.

Defences: Hold a dumbbell only in your defending hand as you go through the exercises for defence. If you are practicing in connection with *gyaku-zuki*, hold dumbbells in both hands. It is best to practice in the *kiba-dachi* position. After doing this, practice a few defences without dumbbells.

A basic principle: If you notice that you are getting slower and losing strength, put the dumbbells aside and practice briefly without dumbbells, quickly and forcefully.

Briefly, here is one more exercise which develops rapid force in the course of striking with your fist.

Stand in the *kiba-dachi* position with your elbows together approximately 4 inches away from your chest, your lower arms and fists together, and your fists at chin level (Illus. 166). From this position, strike blows with your fist, right and then left (Illus. 167), always springing back into the starting position again, with elbows together (Illus. 168). In this, you must aim for a shock effect within a very short distance. Be limber and relax when you practice. Concentrate the tension into the brief moment of striking, and spring back immediately again.

Here is another exercise which does not primarily serve to develop the technique of striking with your fist, but rather increases your endurance: Hold your fists closed loosely in front of your chest. Now strike with the *sanbon-renzuki* which is a triple blow—one upper level blow and two middle level blows. The tempo should be 1 . . . 2, 3. When doing this, the returning fist is brought back in front of your chest. Move naturally (walking around) and strike while you are moving. Do not strike with all your strength but only loosely. You should not strike with force until your breath and movements are co-ordinated. Practice for periods of 5 minutes.

A slight variation which takes somewhat more strength: Stand in the *kiba-dachi* position and strike with the complete *sanbon-renzuki*, i.e., the returning fist goes back to your hip in each case. Strike 600–900 times.

Here is a form of practice for striking with your fist which originated with the fighters from the southern provinces of the Chinese mainland who had "soft" fists: Set up a burning candle firmly at chest level. Stand in front of it in the *gedan-barai* defensive position and then strike quickly and forcefully with *gyaku-zuki*

Illus. 166   Illus. 167   Illus. 168

Exercise to develop fist punching.

(reverse punch) toward the flame of the candle. The point at which you stop your blow should be approximately one inch from the flame. If your blow is loose and quick and comes to an exact stop, the flame will be extinguished by the air pressure. This is a very good exercise, but at the same time a very difficult one. You must be able to combine the soft with the hard. What is required and developed is lightning-fast loose striking and shock-like application of strength at an exactly defined point. This type of practice is usually not as much fun as breaking boards and tiles, striking at real obstacles (hitting posts, sandbags, horses) in order to harden your limbs. Some practitioners of Karate see only the hardness in it and do not understand that the real Karate fighter combines the hard with the soft in his character.

Practice striking toward the candle flame again and again. As you succeed increasingly frequently in "blowing out" the flame, and your movement is relatively effortless, you will have developed a far more dangerous blow with your fist than the person who develops callouses and cartilage at the *makiwara* (hitting post).

Less is more—I mean exercise with understanding and self-control.

One-minute training

This is a form of practice to be carried out at home. I was stimulated to make these experiments because, even after plenty of time, many of my beginning students did not execute the techniques cleanly. They were overwhelmed by the abundance of material to be learned, and they could no longer concentrate their controls on an individual technique when they were practicing. They divided their self-control, and to the same degree the effectiveness of their technique was diminished.

Now I assign "homework" for every day of the week. I undertake only one technique at a time, for example, *soto-uke* (see page 219). I show this technique in detail and explain it exactly. Then I assign the homework. Assume, for example, that this is Monday evening. The homework would be as follows:

For Tuesday: Stand in front of the mirror and carry out the movement of the *soto-uke* slowly and relaxed. Do this for one minute, alternately to the right and to the left.

For Wednesday: Do the same thing with increased self-control.

For Thursday: Continue to carry out the exercise slowly, but put force into the stopping point. Hold it for a second, breathe correctly.

For Friday: Do exactly the same thing with exact control of movement while doing it.

For Saturday: Begin slowly, then continually increase your speed while maintaining exact control.

For Sunday: Carry out the exercise quickly and forcefully.

Practice for just one minute in front of the mirror every day. You will have very good results from this concentrated practice for a week. You really need to practice for only one minute, but this must be completely concentrated. Concentration of effort impresses and imprints the correct execution of this technique and the correct succession of movements in your memory. Neverthe-

Illus. 169.
Class in
defence
practice.

less, this type of exercise should not be done for more than 5 minutes a day because, according to my experience, you no longer keep exactly to the exercise for the day in question, you go beyond it, or tire out your self-control. This "one-minute training," along with the other exercises to be done at home, is especially recommended for advanced students.

All the basic techniques, as they have been described, are practiced in the basic school, the Karate *dojo* or *kihon*. All the pupils line up in rows behind each other according to the colors of their belts, the highest *kyu* or grades to the right facing the instructor. The exercises are practiced by orders (counting) or by the individuals while the instructor (*sensei*) walks by and checks.

It is now absolutely necessary for the advanced Karateka, who

Illus. 170. A class in the sei-za or tai-za position learning correct breathing. This position, resting on heels, allows you to be completely relaxed.

has mastered the individual techniques, to get a feeling of what it is like when a technique strikes and hits its goal with full force. In practicing attacks into empty air, the student cannot get close to the real thing. To overcome this, there is a piece of apparatus called the *makiwara*. This is basically a post which has been wrapped with straw, against which all arm and foot techniques can be practiced. This practice apparatus serves to harden your limbs. Other equipment includes the sandbag for hand and foot techniques, and the horse, an apparatus found in every gym, which is especially suitable for foot techniques. The horse can also be used like a *makiwara*.

With the apparatus you can practice the application of force for the *mae-geri-ke-komi* and *yoko-geri-ke-komi*. Start from all positions—advancing, starting from a turn, and so forth. Doing this will also develop a good eye and how to estimate distance correctly.

A further aid in Karate training is scheduling regular sessions of running. If you force yourself to do this regularly and, if possible, alone, you will soon develop something of the "fighting spirit" you need in Karate. When you run alone, always force yourself to endure even more than if someone were running with you.

However, do not exaggerate at the beginning, but build up to this slowly.

A further exercise which is excellent for learning correct breathing is sitting in the *sei-za* (or *tai-za*) position (Illus. 170). Sit on your heels completely relaxed with the upper part of your body erect (your navel must point slightly upwards). Breathe with your diaphragm. While you are doing this, always be conscious of the middle of your body, the *hara*. Look straight ahead at some point and do not think of anything definite, but rather let thoughts fly through your mind like a breeze. This exercise, if carried out regularly, will also influence your inner attitude very beneficially. However, we will go further into this later.

One of the most important prerequisites for learning true Karate is following a sensible way of life: Moderation in smoking and drinking, sufficient sleep, moderate stimulation (avoid too many movies, too much television and spectator sports). Only a person with a healthy body and mind is capable of concentrating and really learning Karate.

Illus. 171. Karate is a contest of skill between two healthy bodies.

Illus. 172　　　　　　　　　　　　　　　　**Illus. 173**
Back step into gedan-gamae, then forwards into oi-zuki, while your
opponent defends with soto-uke.

6. Contest Exercises
(Kumite)

Up to this point we have only examined the techniques of Karate. Whenever you had a partner, the purpose of his presence was to help you with your exercises. However, Karate is primarily a contest between two fighters. You are confronted by an opponent against whom you must defend yourself and counter-attack. In other words, the basic techniques of this sport are dominated by the knowledge that you are training for an actual Karate combat.

There are various contest (or *kumite*) forms (or *katas*) of exercise:

1. *Kihon-kumite* (basic partner training)
    a) *ippon-kumite*
    b) *sanbon-* and *gohon-kumite*
2. *Jiyu-ippon-kumite* (semi-free sparring)
3. *Jiyu-kumite* (free-style contest)

The main purpose of the contest exercises in *kihon-kumite* and in *jiyu-ippon-kumite* is to train your precision and your eye. Constant training will teach you reflex-conditioned reactions, inducing within you a sense of caution and care. Ideally, in the end you will hardly have to think about these movements and can almost shut out your conscious concentration on them. This ideal state can only be achieved by persistent training. In *kihon-kumite* every attack and every defence is precisely thought out beforehand. Your unconscious precision and your exactitude is developed for use in a free contest.

Ippon-kumite

The partners confront each other in *hachiji-dachi*, the basic position. One partner, the attacker, assumes a distance, i.e., he stretches out both arms (making fists) until they touch his partner's chest. Now he steps back with his right foot (Illus. 172) in the position called *gedan-gamae*. Then he attacks on the right with *oi-zuki* (Illus. 173), for instance at the middle level (announcing it beforehand). His partner turns and steps back with his right foot, defends himself in the process with *soto-uke* (Illus. 173), and in turn counter-attacks with *gyaku-zuki* on the right (Illus. 174).

The announcement by the instructor would sound something like this: Attack *oi-zuki* (simultaneous jab same side), middle

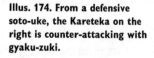

Illus. 174. From a defensive soto-uke, the Kareteka on the right is counter-attacking with gyaku-zuki.

Illus. 175
Soto-uke from inside.

Illus. 176
Counter-attack with shito-uke.

level. Defend *soto-uke* from the outside. Counter-attack *gyaku-zuki*. Of course, it is also possible to defend yourself from inside (back to left and a left defence) or at a right angle, either moving back to left or right and from inside (Illus. 175) or defending yourself from outside with *soto-uke*. You can also counter-attack *empi-uchi* (with elbow), *shuto-uchi* (Illus. 176), *yoko-geri*, etc. It is imperative that you exercise the *kihon-kumite* in as many variations as possible, but precisely and forcefully. Mainly you should make sure that the attacking arm and attacking leg of your partner are hit by your defensive measures before your own attacking limbs are stretched out (and thus frozen). There are two reasons for this:

1. If you wait to be struck by the attacking limbs at the very moment when they are fully stretched, this is precisely the moment when the strike is at its most awesome strength. In order to push or strike the assaulting limb aside, you would need enormous strength.

2. Still more important: If you defend yourself only at the moment when the opponent's attack is at its most powerful, when the limbs are fully stretched and "frozen," your defence will come too late. Timing is decisive.

Consequently you have to be faster with your defence than your opponent with his attack. Always anticipate your opponent's movements. Your opponent's attacking leg or arm must be struck while they are still in motion and "unfrozen." Then your defence will be much more effective and you can knock aside any blow regardless of force.

Sanbon- and gohon-kumite

When performing these exercises your partner attacks three times or five times in a row, either at your middle or upper level. Retreating, you must defend yourself three or five times and after the last attack lead into a forceful counter-attack. Then you are the attacker and the whole procedure is reversed. This exercise demands that your thrusts be speedy, exact and powerful and simultaneously that you take care not to lose your balance. Your partner defending himself must see to it that he repulses your attack with precision.

Beginners must train themselves step by step, with clean and precise movements, attacking and aiming with precision, and defending themselves in like manner.

Sanbon and, more importantly, *gohon* contests are of great significance for the advanced student. The defender must always be able to follow the movements of the attacker as if he were him-self an extension of the attacker. When the attacker stops, the defender must also halt his movements on the spot. When the attacker advances, the defender must move back the same distance, if possible without delay. As long as you keep a certain distance from your opponent throughout the contest you should be safe. The importance of this series of movements cannot be stressed enough.

Therefore, advanced students should always continue to exercise *gohon-kumite*, of course with a slight variation from the novice: movements of advance and retreat should be speedier and more fluid. Infuse these motions with intensified force. As the attacker, increase the effort of your assaults until the last thrust becomes the most powerful. The same applies to the defence. You will soon anticipate the movements of your opponent. You can learn to recognize the intent of your partner the very moment he starts

Illus. 177 (left). A class in Karate is practicing contest techniques. The left row is showing gedan-gamae while the right row remains in hachiji-dachi. Illus. 178 (right). As the left row attacks with zuki at the chudan (middle) level, the right row defends with soto-uke (outer edge of forearm).

to attack you. And this is precisely the aim of the ultimate free contest. You should reach the point where you can sense the attack your partner is planning, not only so that you can prepare yourself, but so that you can anticipate the force and nature of the attack. You should train yourself to such an ideal state that you can "smell out" the attack and react to it automatically without consciously thinking about it or your defensive measures.

Jiyu-ippon-kumite

A further step on the path to this goal is this semi-free sparring form in which the two partners move freely and in all directions as in a free-style contest. Who is to be the attacker and who the defender is decided prior to the contest, as is the form of the attack (for example, *oi-zuki*—lunge punch, same side—middle level). The attacker has to find an opening and gain the right distance from his opponent before the attack begins. The defender has to wait for the attack and be prepared to defend himself immediately. As soon as the attack starts, he must ward it off or evade it and go into a counter-attack. As a result, the roles reverse and the attacker becomes defender. This type of exercise makes great demands on the Karateka. It is an excellent exercise to find the right distance, both in the offensive and defensive stances. The lightning-quick recognition and exploitation of an opening in your opponent's cover will become second nature, as should the quick and forceful application of those techniques which follow from the opponent's movement.

A form of the *jiyu-ippon-kumite* which is still more challenging is the variation in which only the attacker and defender are appointed, and not the form of attack. Before proceeding to the free-style contest a few observations regarding the fighting postures are in order with special emphasis on *jiyu-ippon-kumite* and *jiyu-kumite*.

Contest positions

No contest stance or position is required. You can choose the positions most advantageous to your attack or defence. Stances with tensed muscles are not suitable for these purposes since they prevent effective reflex action and quick movement. Such motions are—as you have seen before—only possible when your muscles are relaxed. Your stance must be loose and natural. Don't move more than necessary. (Illus. 179 and 180 on next page.)

For an attack during *jiyu-ippon-kumite* and *jiyu-kumite*:

Always start out with a "long" attack, i.e., throw the weight of your body behind your punch, leaning forward. These exercises are useful when performing *ippon-kumite* and *sanbon-* and *gohon-kumite*. Catapult yourself all the way to the fore when attacking. When your defending partner does not step back far enough you should be able to break through his defences. You can even deal him such a heavy blow that he falls to the ground (provided that your forward movement emanates from the *hara*).

During the *jiyu-ippon-kumite* go on the offensive as if you intend

Illus. 179. The contest begins but the stance must stay loose and natural.

to hit your opponent. You must concentrate on breaking through with your attack or else your Karate will be unrealistic. Only when you notice that your partner defends himself too late, or not at all, is it time for you to stop so that he is not hit. This is to point out that the correct *jiyu-ippon-kumite* and, of course, especially the *jiyu-kumite* (free-style contest) make great demands on the ability and precision of your technique, and on your unconscious yet assured reflexes—characteristics which can only be achieved by persistent and uncompromising training.

The same principle of the "long attack" is also applicable to the leg-attack. Here, too, your *hara*, your whole body, must be thrown forward. This helps to lend greater force and thrust to

Illus. 180. Practice contest techniques in the gym until you are certain you are attacking with your whole body, your hara.

your attack as well as enable you to take the offensive from a greater and safer distance. In this way, a weak defence can be easily broken. Moreover, even if you should fail to penetrate your opponent's defences with such a leg assault, it still might enable you to come closer to him and to continue the contest without delay by applying your hand techniques. Consequently, there is this basic principle to be remembered in a contest: that in Karate techniques every part of your body has to participate. The starting point and the source of your strength for full-body movements always is the *hara*.

For the free-style contest remember these principles:

Never attack with your arms and legs only, but always employ your whole body (*hara*).

In a free-style contest, only advanced students are welcome.

7. The Contest

Jiyu-kumite, the free-style contest

Illus. 181–184 show positions in a contest.

This is the apex of Karate. But it is a stage reserved only to the Karateka who is willing to apply himself with diligence and tenacity to the hard school of precision and exactness. When performing in a free-style contest, every participant must be in the position to avert and stop even the most powerful of attacks shortly before it reaches its target. Although the path to this final form advances step by step (*kihon*: basic steps; *kihon-kumite*: basic partner exercises; *jiyu-ippon-kumite*: semi-free sparring; *jiyu-kumite*: free-style contest), there are possibilities that you can

Illus. 183. The back kick, ushiro-geri.

take a short-cut and start earlier. Karate is an organic entity and the feeling for this should be aroused in each student starting with his first lesson.

Here are a few preparation exercises for your contest:

You have learned positions and movements, as well as the most important defences and counter-attacks, *oi-zuki* and *gyaku-zuki*. Henceforth whenever you train, carry out your basic partner contest-exercises (*kihon-kumite*). Naturally, at first, your individual techniques will not be imbued with great strength, your movements will lack the necessary speed. But as time progresses, so will you and your exercises. Once you avert and defend yourself against

Illus. 184. The roundhouse kick, mawashi-geri.

Practice for the contest.

an attack, and repulse it with a counter-attack, this will give you a feeling for keeping the right distance from your opponent. It will also prove that you can defend yourself and counter-attack.

Here is another exercise you can begin now: Follow the contest position, the cover, and then place yourself opposite your partner for the contest. Move in a manner befitting the Karateka, i.e., economically, yet lightning-quick. Should your opponent advance on you with a large or sliding step, react at once by moving back still faster. Pay attention to your balance and tense your muscles the moment both feet settle down again on the floor. Keep the upper part of your body upright. It is quite possible that both of you will simultaneously attack and collide. Put up your cover at once and push yourself from your opponent. At this juncture, do not attack or go over to the defence. The exercise itself will help you to develop your Karate movements for the next step in the contest.

This next step would be the *jiyu-ippon-kumite*. Your training for definitive movements and exactness must run concurrently, as when performing in *kihon-kumite*. This point is important to remember: Despite your early contest exercises, never relax in applying your basic and elementary Karate principles. These form the background to everything in this sport. Your progress finally depends on the basic Karate foundation you have developed for yourself.

A few more hints for the free-style contest: Wait until you see an opening in your opponent's cover, then take advantage of it and attack him. You may even induce your opponent to drop his cover:

1. Attack actively by feigning an attack and exploiting the opening in his cover which he drops as a result of his defence-reaction. For instance: (a) Aim your first fist attack at his face. Your opponent will raise his hands in defence and the fist of your other hand will proceed with the real attack, driving home on his solar plexus. Or (b) apply *mae-geri* (forward kick with your foot) to his solar plexus. Your opponent will lower his arms in defence, and you thrust your leg as far forward as possible with a simultaneous *oi-zuki* (pursuit blow) to his face.

2. Attack *passively*: This time you pretend to drop your defences. This will tempt your opponent to proceed with an attack on you. You have waited for this and when it comes, you evade it or defend yourself and go over to a strong counter-attack. This form of contest technique conforms to the true essence of Karate, but it demands great agility and skill, a well-trained eye and a reflex-conditioned self-assurance both in defence and counter-attack.

This is another exercise for the contest which will school you in your unconscious reflex reaction: Form a circle about 5 to 6 yards in diameter with four men standing outside and one inside of it. Only one man may stay inside this circle. The four men on the outside each try to deal a blow to the inside-man's shoulder without the latter observing it. Should one succeed, the man who dealt the blow enters the circle while the other joins the rank of the men outside. The man inside the circle has to recognize the "attacks" at the right time and ward them off with a Karate attack. If he is able to apply a well-aimed strong assault, the outside man against whom it was directed must be removed from the circle. Of course the man on the outside should exert every effort to defend himself against the man inside the circle and still deal the blow to the insider's shoulder. This exercise is only suitable for advanced students with an excellent record in Karate.

A valuable and beautiful form of exercise for the Karate contest is provided by training (*jiyu-ippon-kumite* and *jiyu-kumite*) out-of-doors. The ground does not necessarily have to be even. In the countryside you can select a spot which appears most advantageous to you. It is up to your opponent then to attack you. In this fashion, both partners learn to stand on difficult terrain for attack and defence.

Another hint for contest exercises: If you decide to attack with *oi-zuki* and stand too far away for a sliding step, pull back your front leg behind the other leg by about 12 inches (leaving the weight of your body in front) and propel yourself with one leg to the fore as fast as you can. This attack will come as a great surprise to your opponent.

The next aspect of Karate can only be learned from personal instruction.

Illus. 185

8. The Kata

In the *kata* (Illus. 185) a number of pre-determined defences and attacks are conducted in a fixed order of succession to demonstrate methods of defence, attack and counter-attack. There are about 50 of such *kata*, most of which originated in ancient times. Until about 30 years ago, the *kata* was considered the ideal form of Karate. Only since then have the *kumite* forms and *jiyu-kumite* been developed. Even today Karate championships are divided in two parts: *Kata* tournaments (*kata-shiai*) and contest tournaments (*kumite-shiai*).

In the case of *kata-shiai*, contest evaluators assess the performances of the individual, rather like referees in a figure-skating contest. The overall impression of the individual is appraised, and this is determined by the suppleness of movements, the force and precision of techniques, the dynamics of the entire flexible performance.

Kata is usually required of beginners. Some Karateka regard these exercises as a necessary evil for acquiring their black belts. However, a beautifully executed *kata* always arouses the enthusiasm

of the spectators for its aesthetic and mobile appeal. The harmony
of the motions and the explosive dynamics of the exhibition give
the onlookers, as well as the Karateka, a feeling of tremendous
satisfaction. But this sense of delight and rapture is only shared
by spectators and participants alike provided the *kata* is displayed
as an organic whole. Only by attaining this goal can a performance
really "live." So, whoever views the *kata* as nothing more than
a separated unconnected series of exercises has completely missed
the essential point.

The positions and movements and individual techniques must
be mastered in all their totality of strength and precision. The
kata can, for this reason, be considered excellent basic training
for the development of good Karate technique: balance, self-

assured movements, forceful attacks, precise defences—all these will be improved. No substitute serves as well for the elementary basis of contest training. Since in performing a *kata* several imaginary partners must be attacked and defended against from all directions (Illus. 186), this aspect provides a great proving ground for the application of various techniques in a number of situations and indirectly serves as fine training for the free contest.

However, back to our earlier stipulation: A correct *kata* is an organic whole, not just a joining together of several perfectly executed techniques. This in turn provides us with a few plain hints for our instruction in *kata*.

An organic entity is not something knotted together, but something growing out of a preceding movement. Therefore, beginners should learn the lessons of *kata* before they have mastered the various techniques down to the last iota of perfection and exactitude. Important is the totality of the performance. The sharpening up of the separate techniques will come as time progresses. Any *kata* so acquired will soon assume the essence of "life." Once this lesson has penetrated and become second nature to you, you will not get stuck in the execution of your performance. After all, the subconscious control over your movements is projected in the display of your *kata*.

When you master this predetermined course of movements with almost somnambulistic assurance, you will have gradually

Illus. 187.
Practice for the kata may look like a dance in a trance.

absorbed still another aim of Karate: the exhibition of motions and techniques instinctively with trancelike confidence (Illus. 187).

Therefore, never neglect your *kata*! Make an effort to add as much as possible to this by training constantly.

Here are two more exercises for the *kata*: For muscular co-ordination of the arm, perform your *kata* exercises with dumbbells in your hands; for a strong foundation of the lower part of your body, place a partner on your shoulders and perform all movements and steps of the *kata* this way. After this, reverse the roles.

Once more, do you still pay attention to the fact that your navel must always point slightly up? And that the *hara* serves as the middle of your body? Do you still remember the correct way to brace yourself and tense your muscles as well as to relax by breathing?

9. The Spiritual Basis of Karate

We have now completed the discussion of pure Karate techniques. It is not the end of your learning. This is really the starting point —something we will prove in a little while.

At first a few observations regarding Karate's history: Karate is a Japanese name and means literally "Empty unarmed hand." It is interesting that this art is by no means Japanese in origin as might be suspected from the name. On the contrary, this sport has been known in Japan only since the early 1900's. It was formally introduced to Japan by Gichin Funakoshi, a citizen of Okinawa. On that island, Karate, which originated in China, was fully developed. Ironically, we have to thank the Japanese conquerors of Okinawa in the late 19th century, for they would not allow Okinawan natives to carry arms, forcing them to circumvent the edict by devising and mastering a form of contest without arms.

Furthermore, it is interesting to note that all over Southeast Asia there are many systems of pugilism. The "great-grandfather" of all of these contests is the Chinese form of fisticuffs or boxing, which is still being practiced today in China under the names of "Chuang fa" or "Kung fu" and in China and elsewhere under the name of "Kempo." Karate is simply the best known of these systems. Nevertheless we owe our gratitude to the Japanese for having brought this sport into full bloom.

Let us take a look at the motto of the Japanese Karate Association and adopt it for our own:

"The primary aim in the art of Karate is neither victory nor defeat—the true Karate contestant strives for the perfection of his character."

This proverb shows that the essence of Karate is neither mastering the technique of this sport nor victory over your opponent, but triumph over yourself. It follows that the true nature of Karate serves as a school for life.

"But," you will protest, "doesn't this presuppose that the above words 'to strive for' imply that the student must have good will? What happens then when someone with criminal intentions learns the techniques of this sport?"

To this objection it is best for you to recall: The first things a Karateka must learn are the positions which, to be honest, are and look clumsy and do not make much sense at first. Next follows the rather dull learning period of the various techniques in *kihon* (basic training). This always proves to be a hard course. You have to conquer yourself constantly. You have to concentrate, to approach the techniques with deep understanding and practice incessantly and self-critically. This by itself requires great will power. Such training demands and develops certain characteristics: concentration, an alert mind, will power, self-control, all of which will stand you in good stead throughout life. Karate therefore really is a school preparing you for the challenges in life. All this becomes obvious after a few lessons in this sport. Experience has fortunately shown that when criminal characters are intent on learning the art of Karate with the sole purpose of using the techniques for offensive reasons, they miss the entire point of the basic schooling. For months on end they are not shown "lethal blows" but rather subjected to "senseless" and "awkward" positions and movements. In most cases such scoundrels drop out after several weeks. They don't have the stamina to train themselves.

It is worthwhile to point out once more at this juncture that in a truly understood Karate lesson no real danger exists. It takes a long time to attain ability in Karate.

Learning true Karate (as well as Judo and other contest sports) is of great value. With the aid of a conscientious and responsible

262

instructor, Karate can serve as the backbone for a wholesome outlook on life. It can truly be of great service in your attempt to perfect your character. Naturally, if you do not stick to it and use your will power, you will not prevail. I have discovered, to my great and pleasant surprise that in the course of oral instructions I have given as well as during the period of physical training, many of my students have found within their natures unsuspected reservoirs of will power.

Starting with your first schooling, Karate demands a thorough understanding of and reflection on the psychological reality and regulations of the sport, and furthermore persistent, self-critical training governed by the motto, "Less is more," correctly understood. The characteristics and experiences you gain will be of special value in meeting the requirements of your daily life if you truly understand your Karate lessons and apply them to life. Once your mind no longer has to concentrate consciously on individual movements and techniques, your mind can be considered free, prepared for the challenges of the contest. Only by performing the totality of your motions almost as if "in a trance" can you be certain that your mind is capable of applying your actions with a well-nigh effortless confidence to any given situation. This achievement will imbue you with confidence under all circumstances. You know that regardless of how your opponent attacks, you are in control of all your defences. This inner equanimity—and healthy self-assurance—will prove most rewarding in any situation that might arise in life.

A person matures as he goes through life. Anyone struggling upward over life's obstacles without breaking or capitulating is composed, intelligent and endowed with an inner superiority. Karate looks at these aims as its final goal to be emulated: by perseverance in conquest over your weakness (during the elementary training period) and later in contest with your partner (*kumite*) to aspire to this essential philosophy of life. A person who does not struggle, who does not mentally or psychologically grapple with happenings or things that challenge him day by day has lost something of his human psyche.

This is part of today's sickness. Young people often do not know what to do with themselves, bored as they may be. They plunge from one superficial pastime into another and often end up regarding themselves as pathetic and bored failures. All you have to do is to look at the blank faces in a bar or an amusement arcade where youngsters hang out. The point that strikes you at once is that these youths don't want to do anything on their own—they want to be entertained. When it comes to intelligent conversation or discussion (a contest between minds), they exhibit a complete absence of sensible and meaningful talk.

"Stagnation means boredom, death; aspiration means life." We could be heartless and maintain that the life many people (and by no means merely young people) lead is not really a life for humans, but sheer vegetation, almost inhuman. They think of today, never bother about tomorrow. Their leisure lacks goals, is aimless wandering. Their joy lies in nihilism rather than in the hope for a constructive future.

Against all these attitudes, Karate stands as a philosophy which can help anyone to master life with an inner wholesomeness.

Life is a struggle and only in struggling do humans grow and mature. It is not difficult to understand what the Greek philosopher Heraclitus meant when he said that "War is the father of all things." Along the same line, with a never-rest-on-your-laurels argument, runs Goethe's adage in "Faust" when he has the angels utter the line: "Whoever strives and struggles, him we can liberate."

Once Taiji Kase, 6th Dan (Illus. 188), told me: "Karate is not a shallow sport. You can always probe deeper into it but will never be able to completely plumb its depths." And yet there are many students who claim they know all about Karate once they have managed to master a few of the techniques!

So be cautious! With the mastery of these techniques, only then does the real Karate start. Only then can your mind be truly free, liberated from the conscious clutter of movements. When you have automatic self-assurance and control over your body movements, then you can gain mental and spiritual serenity, adjust completely to life. If you are prepared to take this seriously, then Karate (Judo, etc.) will not only serve as a means to defend yourself in an emergency but, more importantly, as a way to police the physical and mental aspects of your personality. In the final analysis, consequently, you not only defeat your opponent but the weaknesses in yourself.

When you learn to drive a car, your entire attention and concentration at first is focused on various activities: shifting of gears, operating the clutch, brake, and steering wheel; when you first learn to dance you count 1–2–3, step to the left, etc. It is only later, after you have mastered the art of driving or dancing, that you can perform these duties and at the same time converse and joke with your backseat driver or dancing partner. The techniques of braking and the counting of steps have become second nature to you. This is how it should be with your Karate. When your mind has been liberated of technique, it is freed to act subconsciously.

The psyche is like water (misu no kokoro)

The mind should be calm, like a surface of a village pond—serene and ready to ebb away gradually whenever and wherever it is needed. The mirror of the pond's surface reflects everything surrounding it. Thus, you are able to absorb the reflected intent of your opponent; your mind is at your disposal and lets you react instinctively. This swift reaction should relate to all situations, but it is only possible if your mind gets "stuck" nowhere and remains as serene as the water in the pond. What you need is absolute calm and concentration. If your mind swerves for only one second, or fixes upon one aspect only, or if it deliberately occupies itself with, for example, the possibility of an attack, then you may be surprised by a completely unexpected attack from your opponent, merely because your mind was not calm and ready—but was burdened. It was, so to speak, disturbed, just like the ruffled waters of a lake. You know that when the surface of water is rippled by waves it can no longer reflect its surroundings.

Remove yourself at once from any uneasy attitudes. Call the ideal state equanimity if you will. To achieve this state, you will have to train yourself. The novice must practice his techniques with persistent concentration. Even the experts can only retain their mastery of these techniques by continuing their practice year after year. Their minds have to remain free, calm, unencumbered and ready, just like the water of a still pond.

Through years of conscientious training you will attain the exhilarating sensation of self-liberation. You will hardly be aware of the defensive or offensive measures you are using and can adapt yourself to any situation without losing your "cool."

"Due to his self-consciousness Man is frequently converted into a creature of automation," writes E. Hoelker in "Doctor and Sport, the German Medical Weekly." When you no longer fix your thoughts upon a single aim, when you aspire to nothing, want and expect nothing, yet when you know how to utilize your unswerving strength to achieve the possible as well as the impossible—this attitude, because of its unpremeditated and selfless nature, is considered by many masters of Karate as being on the elevated plateau called "spiritual." The mind is saturated with spiritual alertness and is consequently referred to as "correct presence of mind." The mind is ubiquitous, simply because it does not stick to one particular spot, but is everywhere.

A mind is like the moon (tsuki no kokoro)

Moonlight can be seen everywhere, yet it clings nowhere. In like manner you must be conscious of the movements of your opponent; that is, you must be like the moon which looks upon everything yet does not cling to any one spot. Nervousness or the slightest distraction and intimidation resemble the clouds which move in front of the moon.

Naturally you can apply this philosophy to every situation in life, deploying your reservoir of equanimity for each event and using your mental attitude for the correct handling of things. The source and the nature of this mental attitude is *hara* for the Japanese.

The mind may be able to discover an opening in your opponent's stance, but this will be of little avail to you if you lack the will to exploit this situation at once.

General observations about the contest

A lesson you have learned previously is that actual fighting and defence cannot be considered so much a technical as a psychological problem. The best technique, the finest know-how, will let you down if you are not in full control of yourself.

Here are a few reflections which, like earlier ones, not only apply to Karate but to all forms of dual sports. In the chapter dealing with contest positions you were asked to keep your body as loose, limp, relaxed and natural as possible, yet be prepared for all eventualities. "Anyone who is truly prepared does not appear to be prepared at all." You must not show preparedness in the slightest degree although you must be ready for everything.

It is told of old masters of sword fights that throughout the day they moved in such a way as *never* to expose themselves to attack through an opening in their deportment. This of course is the ideal aim for every student of a contest sport: to reach a state of such perfection that your instincts guide you through daily life with a sense of preparedness for all situations.

Your eyes should always level with the eyes of your opponent. The eye is the mirror of the soul. You can thus look "into" your partner and even influence his mental attitude through your own, as reflected in your eyes. Concurrently with this, you can survey each movement of his arms, legs, etc.

The real fighter does not want to fight. He does not ponder victory or defeat. He does not mix in fights, except when an innocent person is in dire need or danger. As long as he hankers after fisticuffs and consciously concentrates only on triumphing over his opponent, he is not fully in possession of the "mind of the water." His mind is too preoccupied and fixed on one direction and, as a result, is not free.

The hara

Now, back to the meaning of *hara*, the focal point of the body, the center of gravity of man, just below the navel. You have already learned about the technical aspects of *hara*, as in posture and breathing. But *hara* also has more meaningful implications.

The end result of our life struggle—as of the true Karate—should be attaining an inner posture or attitude. This attitude is the consequence of your maturing. It means that you have found your crucial point. The symbol of this point is *hara*. It is this concept, this frame of mind, from which all things originate and to which all things return. This spiritual center of gravity relates to the center of gravity of the body, and an understanding of this proves that you have discovered your spiritual as well as physical center. The physical center is the *hara*. The inner posture of a sitting Japanese is as meaningful to him as is his visible posture. The Japanese consequently finds a relaxed yet upright calm within him in all situations of life.

The unifying words, "upright" and "relaxed" are characteristic of this attitude. You will find yourself inwardly completely harmonized and balanced. Upright, cool, steadfast and collected— these are the signs, the characteristics of this spirito-mental posture. The Japanese regards victory in the sense of relating his existence to the total expression of *hara*. Thus, how you stand and sit, so will you walk and dance and act and wrestle. In the same fashion you must also fight "without motion," because every movement is, so to speak, anchored to the immovable center of gravity (the *hara*) from which all movements spring and derive their strength, direction and degree of control.

Once you have discovered the secret of *hara* for yourself, you are no longer so dependent on physical exertion, but can win with a completely different sort of force. *Hara* hides an almost supernatural strength which will inspire you to extraordinary feats of accomplishments in daily life. And since *hara* forms a subconscious background in the everyday life activities of the Japanese, serving them as a basis of inner maturity, they can take advantage of this mysterious strength and draw from it at will to achieve enormous feats in mental and physical performance. With *hara* you keep your presence of mind, in deed and otherwise. Those in possession of *hara* are prepared for every situation, even death. They can bow before the victor, in humility and without shame, and they have the patience to wait.

When you read about practicing, you will think of these actions that help you to master your sport. You will want to perfect your techniques and tactics. Practicing over and over again carries the seed of eventual perfection, which in its turn can help you to become a master, a champion. But the self-confidence that backs your attainments depends on more than merely a perfected ability to do something. Otherwise all you can be said to master is the technique of a thing; you will not have truly mastered yourself.

For instance, if you are easily distracted or intimidated, all your learned techniques and ability will forsake you at a decisive moment.

To exert complete control over yourself requires special practice and this is not just the result of technical know-how, but of your inner character development. In this sort of practice there is no visible effort, but change within. Your mind should not take aim for physical victory but for inner gain.

You will now be able to understand what the Japanese means when he says: "Shooting with an arrow and dancing, decorating with flowers and singing, drinking tea and wrestling—it is all the same." Literally, or visually, this adage has little meaning. No—the Japanese artist aims for the totality of the experience and acting it out. The consequence is that the effort will be child's play and the achievement somehow the result of an inner effortless instinct. Allegorically, this is almost like a tree shedding a ripe apple without being conscious of it. The nucleus of this mental attitude is the imperturbability of the center of gravity in the *hara*. If you recognize the truth of all this, you will be able to conquer yourself and your weaknesses and develop your character. Of course, you must set your mind to the task and draw on your faculties of concentration, your will power and alertness.

The actual *hara* can therefore begin only after the techniques have been learned and become second nature. Plainly, this automatic execution of exercises has an additional value. Ego-fixation can be made to retire, because only if an egotistical attitude no longer plays a major role in your life can perfection and achievement come to its fullest bloom. Comprehending this rule will give you a clearer understanding of the possibilities and strength of yourself, and subsequently help in the execution of every form of activity. In a cultivated *hara*, you are the owner of and master over uncommon strength and dependable precision to perform actions which, failing this *hara*, not even the most perfect skill, the hardest will or the most alert attention could bring about. "Total perfection is possible only with *hara*."

You will develop a number of characteristic faculties by practicing *hara*: Total serenity (equanimity and self-possession), yet at the same time a higher sensitivity and comprehension, as well as a preparedness for every surprise and a capacity for lightning-quick decisions which demand hard-headed judgments.

It is not easy to defeat a person with *hara*, but even if you are knocked down with hard blows, your *hara* will swing you back safely on your feet in no time. *Hara* is your firm anchor, which always enables you to find your "center of gravity" again.

But how can you actually practice the *hara*?

Although we have briefly touched on this problem while discussing the various techniques, let us probe a bit deeper into this most important aspect of Karate.

Stand absolutely relaxed and let your shoulders droop. Prepare the lower part of your abdomen for an opponent's thrust without being overly tense. Just let this thought go through your mind: "I am strong. I feel an important part of myself in this lower region, just below the navel." Once you have accepted this concept you will feel quite different, inwardly released and relaxed, upright and serene.

The decisive factor for the attainment of this is equalization of the concepts of tension and relaxation within yourself.

Combined with this concept, of course, is correct breathing.

Illus. 189. The tai-za position, the best for practicing breathing.

Your breathing, under the right controls, comes from your diaphragm. Be quite conscientious about the practicing of your breathing. Practice while sitting down and best of all in the *tai-za* position (Illus. 189). Persisting in this exercise will help you to find your way to practicing *hara*. Sit like this every day for half an hour, inhale and exhale with your diaphragm and put some strength in your abdominal region. Breathe through your nose and keep your mouth closed. Exhale very slowly, but not all the way, so that you can still utter a few words without having to inhale. As you exhale, try to add some strength to your abdomen. When you inhale do it in one brief heave. Yet never force your breathing, let it flow peacefully. As time progresses, you will be able to breathe like this about 10 times per minute; do not attempt to do more; in fact, if you can cut down on the number of exhalations per minute, so much the better. Soon you will reach the point where your respiration flows quite smoothly, almost instinctively. This is an indication that you are well on the way to developing your *hara* fully.

It goes without saying that *hara* must be performed in every posture. Regardless of whether you stand, sit or are otherwise occupied, always make sure that your navel points slightly upward.

This concludes the study of Karate. It is important to realize that the pointers on these pages have emphasized that Karate is not purely a test of physical strength, but that—like Judo, Aikido and other Japanese contest arts—it imbues you with an inner equanimity.

It is to be hoped that every Karateka will devote himself as intensively and selflessly to the mental-spiritual side of the sport as to its techniques, because only by relying on every facet of Karate can you fully benefit from it.

POSITIONS AND MOVEMENTS TO LEARN

Stances

Kake-dachi

Uchi-hachiji-dachi

Sanchin-dachi

Hand techniques

Morote-tsuki

Ura-tsuki

273

Hand techniques (continued)

Mawashi-tsuki

Tate-tsuki

Yama-tsuki

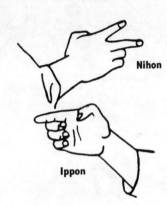

Nihon

Ippon

Strike techniques

Uraken-uchi, downwards

Uraken-uchi, sidewards

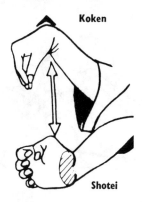

Koken

Shotei

Wrist snap, downwards and upwards

Koken-uchi

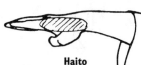

Haito

Shotei-uchi

Haito-uchi, from out in

Haito-uchi, from in out

Foot techniques

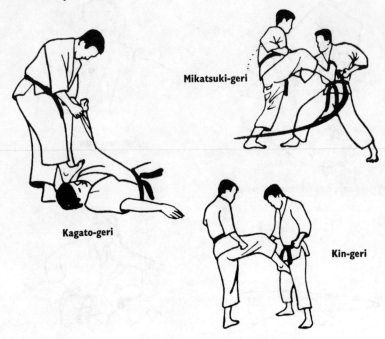

Mikatsuki-geri

Kagato-geri

Kin-geri

Arm defences

Koken-uke

Shotei-uke

Juji-uke defence at the gedan (lower) level against a kick attack.

Morote-uke

Use of leg to defend

Nami-ashi

Mikatsuki-geri-uke

PART III

kempo

Kempo is a sport, a physical exercise and a method of self-defence. With its punching, striking and kicking techniques, Kempo features easy-to-learn ways of escape from all common holds. Kempo can apply in almost any self-defence situation.

INTRODUCTION

With Judo at the height of its popularity and public acceptance, and Karate rapidly closing the gap, the ancient art of Kempo is experiencing a sudden and accelerated growth of interest among teen-agers, students and adults who are seeking another form of self-defence.

The Japanese style of Karate, as practiced today, appears to have descended from the Chinese art of Ch'uan-fa, while Kempo or the "fist way" owes its development to some of the Ju-jitsu schools that flourished in the days of the Japanese samurai.

According to *Kokumin Hyakka Jiten,* the Japanese encyclopedia published in 1966 by the Heibonsha firm, Kempo's origin is rooted within the old Ju-jitsu *ryus,* or schools, such as the Sekeguchi, Shibukawa, Kito, Jikishin, and the Tenshin-Shinyo. Some schools taught the special weapons techniques of Yawara for self-defence; others preferred Tai-jitsu with its grappling and throwing forms, or Kempo, which stresses punching, striking and kicking techniques.

In the year 1659, a Chinese named Cheng Tsu U arrived in the province of Edo. While staying at the Kokuseyi temple, Cheng Tsu U impressed the observant samurai with demonstrations of his art, which resembled pugilism. During the latter part of the 16th century, the Kempo aspect of Ju-jitsu had become formalized into a distinct system of self-defence, employing both hand and weapons techniques. Between the 17th and early 19th centuries, additional *ryus* teaching various self-defence techniques came into existence. In this period all self-defence forms were referred to as Ju-jitsu. Today, Kempo, like its sister arts, is a sport, a physical exercise, and a means of self-defence.

Throughout the following pages, the basic Kempo techniques, as used in contemporary Japan, are presented. For the most part, the techniques were chosen on the basis of practical application and easy execution. The text is designed for the student of martial arts who has already received training in basic defence fundamentals, and to those seeking additional self-defence techniques. However, it is quite likely that the average individual, with experience and training, may effectively apply many of these techniques in emergencies where he (or she) is threatened with bodily harm.

PHOTO 1.　　　　　　　　PHOTO 2.

Before You Begin

A good stance is essential for smooth execution of self-defence techniques and body balance. The two most frequently used stances are the forward and straddle-leg stance.

Right Forward Stance—(Photos 1 and 2)

Start from a natural standing position with feet about 10 inches apart. Lower your body balance by bending at the knees and stepping forward with your right leg. Simultaneously push off the stationary leg. Keep your back straight and both feet flat on the ground. About 60 per cent of the body weight is placed on the front leg and 40 per cent on the rear leg which is kept fully extended and tense. To move into a left forward stance, simply step forward with the left leg and push off with the right.

Often, one is forced to fall back into a forward stance to avoid a sudden attack coming directly from the front. To move backwards into a right forward stance, leave your right foot stationary and slide the left foot back into position.

Straddle-leg Stance—(Photos 3 and 4)

This is a strong stance from the side and is used mainly when delivering a counter-attack after first dodging your opponent's initial attack. Keep your feet flat on the ground with the toes pointing directly ahead, and legs spread apart almost twice the width of your shoulders. The muscles of hips and legs are tensed. Exert pressure outwards, knees bent and back straight.

PHOTO 3.   PHOTO 4.

Basic Kempo Stance—(Photos 5 and 6)

The Kempo stance is a variation of the forward stance and is used when greater flexibility is desired than is possible with the more rigid forward stance. Both knees are bent; the front foot is turned slightly inward to give the groin area better protection against a possible kick.

PHOTO 5.   PHOTO 6.

PHOTO 7.　　　　　　　　PHOTO 8.

Knife-hand Block—(Photos 7 and 8)

This is the most important and extensively used blocking technique. To form the knife-hand (to make your hand resemble a knife), keep four fingers close together, the heel of your palm flat, your thumb bent and pressed outwards. The edge of your hand on the little finger side is employed to deflect the attacker's blows or to strike back at the neck and face. Raise your hand to the opposite ear (palm facing the ear) and slash downwards with a counter-clockwise twisting motion of the wrist. Use your elbow as a pivot. Keep your wrist rigid and straight. Although the knife-hand block is generally employed to deflect blows to the chest and neck areas, it is often used to protect the head and the groin targets.

Double Knife-hand Block—(Photo 9)

This is a specialized block against a weapon such as a club. By stepping in with a straddle-leg stance, both hands can be used to block the roundhouse type of a weapons attack. After the block, the outside blocking hand (farthest away from the attacker) grasps the attacker's weapon hand at the wrist, and a blow is delivered to the face or groin with the other hand.

284

PHOTO 9.

PHOTO 10.

Front Snap Kick—(Photo 10)

The knee is brought up sharply and the snapping upwards motion of the foreleg is utilized to kick the attacker's groin, solar plexus, or chin. This kick is usually executed from the forward stance.

Side Thrust Kick—(Photo 11)

The knee must be brought up as in the front kick and thrust out, directly sideways like a punch. The kick is used against the attacker's groin, ribs, and face. Either the forward or the straddle-leg stance may be used.

Photo 11.

Photo 12.

Photo 13.

Roundhouse Kick—(Photo 12)

Your bent leg is raised sideways and swung forward in a circular motion like a roundhouse punch so that the ball of your foot strikes the ribs, neck, or face of your opponent.

Flying Side Kick—(Photo 13)

This is the side thrust kick, executed after leaping into the air. It is used to attack the opponent's neck and face. As it is a specialized technique, a great deal of repetition and exercise is normally required to execute it properly.

PHOTO 14. *The attacker grips your throat with both hands.*

1. Defence against front choke

The attacker has seized your throat with both hands (Photo 14). Raise your right arm straight overhead while pivoting back into a straddle-leg stance (Photo 15) and bring your arm down and across the attacker's forearms (Photo 16). With the same hand deliver a knife-hand strike to his neck or eyes (Photo 17) and follow through with a fist blow to the attacker's mid-section (Photo 18).

To illustrate more realistically the proper application of this typical self-defence technique, Photos 19, 20, 21, 22, and 23 have been posed in civilian attire.

PHOTO 15. *Upraise arm like a sword.*

PHOTO 16. *Sweep sword-hand across your attacker's forearms.*

PHOTO 17.   *Knife-hand strike to his neck or eyes.*

PHOTO 18.   *Thrust punch to his mid-section.*

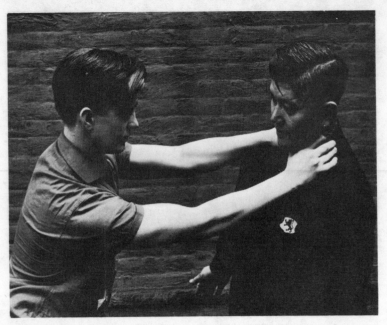

Photo 19.   *The attacker grips your throat with both hands.*

The defence against the front choke is repeated in this sequence of photos. Civilian attire and a realistic setting have been used to help create the everyday circumstances in which a situation of this nature might occur. Note that the movements are the same and equally effective.

PHOTO 20. *Upraise arm like a sword.*

PHOTO 21. *Sweep sword-hand across your attacker's forearms.*

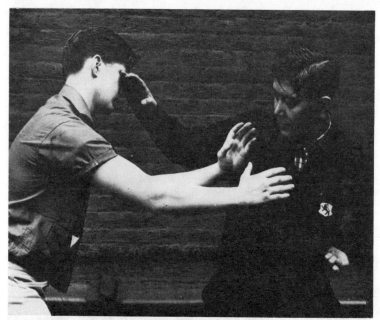

PHOTO 22. *Knife-hand strike to his neck or eyes.*
PHOTO 23. *Thrust punch to his mid-section.*

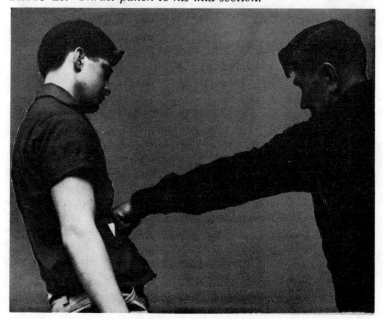

PHOTO 24. *The wrist grab.*

2. Defence against cross-wrist grab

If the attacker seizes your right wrist with his right hand in an attempt to forcibly pull you off balance (Photo 24), step forward and to the outside with your left foot. Bend your arm at the elbow in a circular clockwise motion so that your fingers are pointed straight up (as shown from the opposite side in Photo 25). Pivot completely around now on your left foot until you are facing in the same direction as your attacker (Photo 26). Sharply deliver a knife-hand blow to his ribs with your left hand (Photo 27) to break his hold.

Photo 25. *Keep elbow of captured arm close to body. Swing hand upwards in a circular, clockwise motion. Keep fingers pointed straight up.*

PHOTO 26. *Pivot and face in the same direction as your attacker. Turn your right wrist (palm down) and grasp attacker's right wrist while maintaining a straddle-leg stance.*

PHOTO 27.   *Knife-hand strike to the ribs. A strong straddle-leg stance must be kept to ensure good balance and striking power from the side.*

PHOTO 28. *The double-wrist grab.*

3. Defence against double-wrist grab

Both of your wrists have been seized by the attacker (Photo 28). Spreading your arms outwards, lower your body and execute a front kick to your attacker's groin (Photo 29), which will make him double up.

PHOTO 29.   *Lower your body and spread your arms to your sides. Snap kick sharply to attacker's groin with either foot.*

Photo 30. *Off-balance attempt by attacker.*

3-A. Variation of defence against double-wrist grab

When your attacker forcibly attempts to pull you forward (Photo 30), step towards him into a forward stance. Keep your left arm fully extended while thrusting at his eyes in a clockwise circular movement with your right knife hand (Photo 31).

PHOTO 31. Step forward quickly into a forward stance to utilize attacker's pulling motion to your advantage, and attack his eyes with a knife-hand thrust.

PHOTO 32. *Attempted lapel grab.*

PHOTO 33. *Smash fists down on attacker's forearms.*

4. Defence against double-lapel grab

Your attacker attempts to seize your lapels with both hands (Photo 32). Smash down sharply on his forearms with your fists (Photo 33) and then deliver a double back-fist strike to his eyes (Photo 34). Follow up with your right knee to his groin (Photo 35).

PHOTO 34. *Double back-fists to his eyes.*

PHOTO 35. *Knee thrust to his groin.*

PHOTO 36. *The approach.*

5. Defence against bearhug

In an attempted bearhug (Photo 36), the attacker encircles both your arms and tries to bend you backwards (Photo 37). Step back quickly into a forward stance while thrusting both fists strongly into your attacker's mid-section, followed by a knee-smash to his groin (Photo 38).

Photo 37. Double punch to the mid-section.

Photo 38. Knee thrust to the groin.

Photo 39. *If your arms are free, employ thumb gouge to the eyes with both hands and follow up with knee-groin smash to break attacker's hold on waist.*

5-A. Variation of defence against bearhug

Should the attacker encircle your waist with his arms, leaving your arms free, simply employ the thumb-eye gouge and the knee-groin smash to break his hold (Photo 39).

PHOTO 40. *Shift weight forward; smash down on attacker's head with both hands and drive knee into attacker's face to foil dive-tackle attempt.*

6. Defence against dive-tackle

Should the attacker suddenly dive for your legs at close range, shift your weight forward. At the same time, smash his head down with both hands and strongly thrust your knee into his face (Photo 40).

PHOTO 41. *Step back and to the outside and strike at attacker's neck.*

6-A. Variation of defence against dive-tackle

Another effective method of evading the dive-tackle is shown in Photos 41 and 42. Quickly drop back into a forward stance at a 45° angle to the outside. Hit the attacker's neck with double knife-hand strikes and smash down on the attacker's spine or neck with your elbow.

PHOTO 42. *Bring elbow straight down at base of the neck or spine and smash the attacker to the ground.*

PHOTO 43. *The attempted shoulder armlock from the side.*

7. Defence against arm hold from the side

In Photo 43, the attacker is about to execute the painful shoulder armlock. To prevent this, move sideways towards him into a straddle-leg stance while directing an elbow thrust at his ribs (Photo 44). To force him to the ground, place your inside leg tightly against his, and press your knee forward strongly into the back of your attacker's knee (Photo 45).

Photo 44. *Sideward elbow smash.*

Photo 45. *Press forward hard at your attacker's knee.*

PHOTO 46. *The side headlock in effect.*

8. Defence against headlock from the side

The side headlock is a powerful, punishing hold. You must act quickly to prevent your attacker from employing its crushing leverage. If your attacker is right-handed, move in immediately to his right side (Photo 46). Attack his eyes with your left hand (Photo 47) while your right hand reaches from behind his right leg to his crotch. Lift with your right arm and push with the left towards his rear to throw him (Photo 48). Follow up quickly with a knee-smash to his ribs or a fist blow to his face (Photo 49).

PHOTO 47. *Push back with your left hand and lift up with your right.*

PHOTO 48. *The attacker loses his balance and tumbles backwards.*

PHOTO 49. *Follow up quickly with a knee smash to the attacker's ribs or a fist blow to his face.*

314

PHOTO 50. *Hammerlock attempt.*

9. Defence against hammerlock

If the attacker seizes and tries to twist your right arm behind you (Photo 50), resist immediately by pushing down hard with your captured hand. At the same time, swing your body inwards to your left, pivoting sharply on your right foot (Photo 51) while striking your attacker's jaw or face with your left elbow. Follow through with an instep kick on his right foot with your left heel. Continue your pivot to the outside and hit your attacker's throat with your left (knife) hand (Photo 52). Throw your attacker to the ground by sweeping his injured foot forward, and deliver a fist blow to his face (Photo 53).

PHOTO 51. *Pivot sharply on your right foot towards your left and strike attacker's jaw with your left elbow.*

PHOTO 52. *Knife-hand slash to his throat.*

PHOTO 53. *Thrust punch to his face.*

PHOTO 54. *Rear bearhug attempt.*

10. Defence against rear bearhug

In the rear bearhug, the attacker encircles your arms from behind and tries to pin them to your sides (Photo 54). Immediately lower your body and at the same time force your elbows outwards and upwards to loosen his hold (Photo 55). Twist your body sideways and step forward with your left foot while striking his groin with your right (knife) hand (Photo 56). Assume a strong straddle-leg stance and deliver a sideward elbow strike to your attacker's mid-section (Photo 57), followed by a circular clawing movement to his eyes with your left hand (Photo 58).

PHOTO 55. *Force elbows outwards.*

PHOTO 56.
Knife hand to attacker's groin.

319

PHOTO 57.
*Sideward elbow
smash from
straddle-leg stance.*

PHOTO 58.
*Clawing attack
on his eyes.*

320

PHOTO 59. *The full nelson hold being applied. Clamp your arms tightly against the attacker's to prevent him from moving them up further.*

11. Defence against full nelson

The full nelson, once applied, is a difficult hold to break. At the very instant the attacker slides his arms under yours, clamp your arms tightly against his. This will prevent him from moving his arms up further (Photo 59). Stamp down hard on his instep with your heel (Photo 60). Now place your kicking foot about eight inches in front of you (Photo 61) and swing your other foot around and behind your attacker, while still keeping his arms trapped. Drive him backwards with a sideward elbow smash to his jaw or throat (Photo 62).

321

PHOTO 60. *Stamp down hard on attacker's instep.*

PHOTO 61. *Swing around attacker's injured foot.*

322

Photo 62. *Smash to his face with your right elbow to drive him backwards.*

PHOTO 63. *Drive your heel down on attacker's instep.*

12. Defence against rear strangle

The attacker has succeeded in wrapping his arm around your throat from behind in a choking attempt. Lower your body and drive your right heel down hard on his right instep while pulling him forward with both hands (Photo 63). Then drop to your right knee and place your right leg tightly against his right ankle. Keep your left leg well braced (Photo 64). Continue pulling forcibly on his captured arm towards your left and throw him over your right shoulder (Photo 65). Follow through with a (right) knife-hand strike between his eyes (Photo 66).

Photo 64.
The throwing position.

Photo 65.
*Pull hard to the left
on his captured arm.*

Photo 66. *Follow through with a knife-hand strike between the eyes at the bridge of his nose.*

Photo 67. *Both wrists seized from behind.*

13. Defence against double-wrist grab from behind

Both of your wrists have been seized from behind by an
attacker who forcibly pulls you down and back to prevent you
from employing a kicking technique against him (Photo 67).
Using your right foot as a pivot, swing around towards your left
into your opponent, bringing your left hand up and around in a
circular, counter-clockwise motion (Photo 68). Now step forward
strongly, bringing your left foot into a forward stance, and
thrust sharply at your attacker's eyes with your left (knife) hand
(Photo 69). Bring up your right knee into his groin (Photo 70).

PHOTO 68. *Swing around, using your attacker's force against him.*

PHOTO 69. *Knife-hand thrust to his eyes.*

Photo 70. *Follow up with the right knee smash to his groin.*

PHOTO 71. *The knee block.*

14. Defence against front kick

If an attacker attempts a front kick to your groin with his right foot, bring your right knee up quickly, angled slightly towards the middle of your body to block his kick (Photo 71). The knee block is very useful if, for any reason, you are unable to use your hands to block his kick.

Photo 72. *Side-stepping block.*

14-A. Variation of defence against front kick

If an attacker attempts to kick you with his right foot (Photo 72), quickly step diagonally sideways into a right, forward stance as he moves, while sweeping away his foot with your left forearm. Immediately shift your body to the opposite direction into a left forward stance and strike the attacker's body with your right fist (Photo 73).

Photo 73. *Thrust punch to body.*

PHOTO 74. *Move in while deflecting attacker's blow.*

15. Defence against fist blow

Assume the basic Kempo stance when an attacker threatens you with his fists. Meet his right-hand punch by sliding forward with both feet, and at the same time deflect his blow with a left inside forearm block (Photo 74). Follow through with a straight thrust fist blow with the same hand to your attacker's jaw or face (Photo 75).

Should the attacker move in with his left hand, use your right hand to parry and counter while stepping backwards into a right basic Kempo stance.

Photo 75.   *After deflecting your attacker's first blow, use the same hand to deliver a straight punch to his head.*

PHOTO 76. *Lower your body quickly.*

16. Defence against rear hip throw

An attacker wraps his arms around your waist from behind in an attempt to dash you to the ground (Photo 76). Lower your body quickly and snap your left or right heel up hard into his groin (Photo 77).

PHOTO 77. *Heel kick to the groin. Snap your right heel up sharply into his groin.*

PHOTO 78. *Your arms are held by two attackers.*

17. Defence for use when arms are held by two attackers

Two attackers have seized your arms from either side and are attempting to pull them in opposite directions (Photo 78). Resist their pull by bending your wrists sharply inwards while cross-stepping with your left foot towards the attacker on your right. This will, in effect, make the attacker on your right help you pull away from the attacker on your left (Photo 79). Now bring your right heel down hard on the instep of the attacker on your right (Photo 80), and in the same motion turn and deliver a right front kick to the other attacker's groin (Photo 81).

PHOTO 79. *Cross-step with your left foot.*

PHOTO 80. *Heel thrust to attacker's instep knocks him down.*

Photo 81. *Front kick to the groin takes care of second attacker.*

PHOTO 82. *An attack by grabbing and punching.*

18. Defence against grabbing and punching attack

An attacker has suddenly seized your lapel with his right hand in an attempt to strike your face with his left (Photo 82). Quickly twist your body sideways by withdrawing your left foot directly to the rear, while sharply thrusting your right palm heel out and upwards right into the base of his nose (Photo 83). After executing the palm-heel strike with your right hand, pivot completely around on your right foot and withdraw your left leg to the rear so that you are now facing in the same direction as your attacker. (In Photos 84, 85, and 86, the camera has been moved so that you can see the positions of attacker and defender better during the throwing technique which follows.) As you pivot, hold tightly to his left wrist or sleeve (Photo 84). Now lean forward in a low forward stance, and grasp his upper left arm with your right hand. Push hard against him with your right elbow while pulling strongly with your left arm (Photo 85). The sudden change of direction of your counter-attack will cause your attacker to lose his balance and fall. Follow through with either a kick or a knife-hand strike (Photo 86).

PHOTO 83. *Palm-heel thrust to attacker's face.*

PHOTO 84. *Pivot into throwing position. (Positions of attacker and defender have been changed to better illustrate the throwing technique.)*

Photo 85.   *The throw.*

Photo 86.   *Follow-up position.*

PHOTO 87. *Knife-hand block of club attack.*

19. Defence against roundhouse club attack

An attacker has attempted a roundhouse club assault on your head (Photo 87). Block his club hand with a left extended knife-hand block while stepping directly back towards your rear. Lean slightly backwards. After the block, immediately seize his right wrist or sleeve with your left hand and counter with a left side thrust kick to your attacker's head or throat (Photo 88). Follow this with a roundhouse kick with your right foot to his head (Photo 89).

PHOTO 88.   *Side thrust kick to attacker's head.*

PHOTO 89.   *Roundhouse kick to his face.*

PHOTO 90.   *Double forearm block of club attack.*

20. Defence against downward slash with a club

To avoid being hit by a downward slashing club held in the attacker's right hand, step with your right leg directly to your right, while twisting your upper body sideways towards your attacker and blocking the attacker's arm with both forearms (Photo 90). Seize his right sleeve or wrist with your left hand and execute a right knife-hand blow to his face or neck (Photo 91), followed by a front kick to his groin (Photo 92).

PHOTO 91. *Knife-hand strike to attacker's neck or side of his face.*

PHOTO 92. *Front kick to his groin after knife-hand strike to attacker's neck or face.*

PHOTO 93. *Start of club attack against the knees.*

21. Defence for club attack against your knees

A successful club attack to the knees can cripple and leave the victim helpless (Photo 93). If your attacker swings the club with his right hand, step back with your left foot into a half-turn while lifting your right knee straight up to avoid being struck by the club (Photo 94). Simultaneously deliver a side thrust kick to your attacker's face or head (Photo 95).

Photo 94.   *Lift your knee straight up to avoid the blow.*

Photo 95.   *Thrust kick to attacker's face.*

Photo 96. *Overhead club attack.*

22. Defence against overhead club attack

An attacker with a club is about to aim a blow at the top of your head with his right hand (Photo 96). Raise your left arm straight up, pressed tightly against your own face (Photo 97). At the same time, step directly ahead with your left foot into a forward stance (Photo 97), keeping your back straight. The object is to use your upraised left arm as a shield, and make the club and the attacker's arm slide downwards along it, avoiding your head (Photo 98). Simultaneously execute a palm-heel strike just beneath your opponent's nose at a 45° angle with your right hand (Photo 99). Follow through with a right knee smash to your attacker's groin (Photo 100).

Photo 97. *Step forward using your upraised arm as a shield.*

Photo 98. *Arm deflects club.*

350

PHOTO 99. *Simultaneously deliver a palm-heel thrust to attacker's face.*

PHOTO 100. *Knee smash to his groin.*

PHOTO 101.   *The start of a side-arm club attack.*

23. Defence against side-arm club attack

Against an attack from a club wielded side-arm (Photo 101), step forward quickly with your right foot and stop the attacking arm with a double knife-hand block (Photo 102). Now grasp your attacker's arm with both hands while executing a tight circular pivot with your right foot (Photo 103). Lower your body and throw your attacker by pulling him hard in a counter-clockwise motion (Photo 104). It is essential to keep your body tight against his to avoid being struck by the club. After he is down, continue holding his right wrist or sleeve with your left hand. Strike his face with your right fist (Photo 105).

Photo 102. *Double knife-hand block.*

PHOTO 103. *The circular pivot.*

PHOTO 104. *Pull hard on attacker's arm with both hands in a tight circular pivot and use his own force to throw him.*

355

PHOTO 105. *Follow up with a fist blow to the face.*

PHOTO 106. *The straight knife thrust.*

24. Defence against straight knife thrust

When the attacker attempts a straight knife thrust (Photo 106) to your mid-section with his right hand, extend your left arm (Photo 107) and pivot completely around on your left foot outside of his attacking arm (Photo 108). This will deflect the knife thrust away from your body. Do not bend or raise your blocking arm. Now seize your attacker's right wrist with your right hand and hit his ribs with a left knife-hand strike (Photo 109). Next, with the same hand, deliver a knife-hand slash to your attacker's eyes (Photo 110) and throw him backwards with a downward forefinger-and-thumb gouge on his eyes.

PHOTO 107. *Pivot while deflecting the knife thrust.*

PHOTO 108.   *Face in the same direction as your attacker.*

PHOTO 109.   *Seize attacker's weapon hand at the wrist with your right hand and quickly deliver a knife-hand strike to the ribs with your left hand.*

PHOTO 110. *Hit him between the eyes at the bridge of his nose with a knife-hand strike and employ an eye gouge to throw attacker backwards.*

PHOTO 111. *Overhead knife thrust (coming from left).*

25. Defence against overhead knife attack

Careful timing is essential in any form of knife defence. Just as
the attacker moves forward (Photo 111), step slightly forward
and to the outside of his attacking arm with your left foot and
execute a left open-hand sweeping block against his right arm
anywhere from above the elbow (Photo 112) to just below his
shoulder. It is very dangerous to attempt to deflect his forearm
since that part of his arm is moving much faster and is far more
flexible. Now push your attacker's upper arm hard while continuing your pivot clockwise towards his rear. Grasp his right
wrist with your right hand and strike his ribs with your left
knife-hand (Photo 113). Follow through with a knife-hand strike
on his captured arm at the elbow (Photo 114) and force him to
the ground by exerting pressure on his elbow (Photo 115).

361

PHOTO 112. *Pivot to the outside and apply an open-hand pushing block against attacker's upper arm. (To better illustrate the technique, the positions of the attacker and defender have been reversed.)*

362

PHOTO 113. *Grasp his weapon hand at the wrist with your right hand and hit his ribs sharply with a left knife-hand strike.*

PHOTO 114. *Knife-hand strike to the elbow.*

PHOTO 115. *Smash down hard on attacker's arm.*

PHOTO 116. *Using a short stick against a knife.*

26. Use of club or short stick against a knife

With a knife in his right hand, an attacker leaps forward in an attempt to stab or slash at your lower body. Maintain a good grip on your club handle with your right hand (Photo 116). Immediately side-step to the outside of his attacking hand and strike his wrist sharply with a downward slash of your club (Photo 117). Next, strike his face or throat with a sideward club blow (Photo 118).

Photo 117. *Downward slash on attacker's wrist.*

Photo 118. *Sideward club strike to his face.*

PHOTO 119. *An attacker is about to grab a woman.*

27. Defence against grabbing attempt

An attacker approaches you with obvious intent to grab you (Photo 119). Quickly twist your body sideways by withdrawing your left foot directly to the rear (Photo 120). At the same time, sharply thrust your right palm heel out and upwards right into the base of his nose (Photo 121). While your attacker is recovering, give him a quick sharp kick in his groin (Photo 122) and grasp his left wrist or sleeve. Now lean forward in a low forward stance and grasp his upper left arm with your right hand while pulling strongly with your left arm. The sudden change of direction of your counter-attack will cause him to lose his balance. To help him fall, drop your left knee and throw him over your right knee (Photo 123). This is actually a variation of self-defence technique No. 18. You may often adapt and vary the self-defence techniques illustrated in this book according to the problem.

PHOTO 120. *He grabs.*

PHOTO 121.
He runs into a
palm-heel thrust
at the base of
his nose.

PHOTO 122.   *And a front kick to the groin.*

PHOTO 123. *Finally, he is downed with a knee-drop throw.*

PHOTO 124. *Deflecting a straight thrust.*

28. Bo-jitsu

Also a part of Kempo, Bo-jitsu made use of the "bo," or the wooden stick of various lengths, and was often used for self-defence in ancient times. Photos 124, 125 and 126 illustrate how the long stick was used in self-defence.

PHOTO 125. *Blocking a low blow to the knees.*
PHOTO 126. *Side blow to the body.*

PART IV

judo

There is no mystery in Judo—a small man can throw a big man simply by knowing how. Starting with the traditions of Judo, the uniform and the belts, this section prepares you for "the gentle art" with methods for applying your strength, catching your opponent off balance, getting holds, making breakfalls properly—in fact, all the special Judo techniques. By the time you finish this book you will want to be polite to everyone, since you know you can handle any physical combat successfully.

Primitive combat

1. The Sport of Judo

In every region of the world, there is some form of unarmed combat which has sprouted from primitive roots. Through the years, geographical and cultural influences have shaped these forms of combat into the contact sports we know today. Boxing and wrestling are present-day, Western-world developments of unarmed combat.

In Japan, a form of unarmed combat emerged which is more than a contact sport. It teaches not only contest proficiency, but develops the mind and the body—following a strict moral code. It is a sport, a physical culture, a philosophy, known as Judo, "the gentle art."

Judo was developed by Professor Jigaro Kano. At the age of 18, the professor began a long, intensive study of Jujitsu—an ancient method of unarmed combat practiced by Japanese

Two contestants

Beginning a match

warriors. "Not only did I find Jujitsu interesting, but I also realized it was most effective for the training of both body and mind. So by taking together all the good points I had learned of the various schools and adding my own inventions and discoveries, I devised a new system for physical culture and moral training . . . as well as winning contests." This is how Professor Kano described the birth of Judo.

Along with nine students, he established the Kodokan school in Tokyo in 1882 to develop the science of Judo. Today, Kodokan Judo is practiced all over the world. The Kodokan actively directs techniques, safety, and instruction of Judo wherever it is practiced.

Judo, though evolved from Jujitsu, is not intended to be a crippling form of combat. It is a sport—to be studied and played according to the rules and ceremonies of the Kodokan. Kodokan translated means: "A school of studying the 'way'." The "way" is the practice of using maximum efficiency and minimum effort to overcome an opponent. This book is an introduction to the "way."

376

As a Judoka, or Judo player, you must know how to wear the Judo uniform. This uniform, or Judogi, is composed of three pieces—trousers, jacket, and belt.

The trousers, made of heavy cotton, are reinforced at the knees and have a loop at the waist. They are loose-fitting and should extend at least halfway between your knees and ankles.

After you have put on the trousers, pull the drawstring out sideways to tighten the waistband.

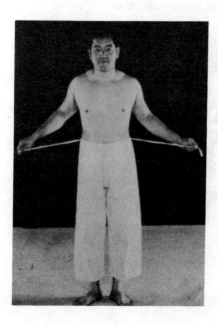

377

Pass one end of the draw-string through the loop of the trousers, then pass the other end through the loop. Tie the ends of the draw-string into a bow knot.

Now, put on the jacket and bring the right side loosely across the body. Cross the left side of the jacket over the right side so that the lower edge is parallel with the waist. The sleeves of the Judogi are loose-fitting, and should extend halfway between the elbow and wrist.

The Judogi belt should be long enough to encircle your body 2½ times. First, grasp the belt in the middle and pass it around your waist from front to rear, so that it crosses in the middle of your back. Next, bring both ends around to the front.

Cross one side of the belt, either right or left, over the other at the waist. Tuck the end of the belt, which is in front of the crossover, under both loops. Now tie both ends into a loose square knot. Tighten the knot by pulling both ends of the belt. This completes your dress.

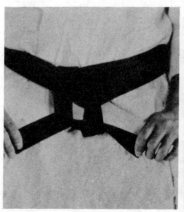

Watching the Judoka

The Judo hall is a place for culture. You must conduct yourself in a serious manner at all times. Idle banter and noisy actions have no place in Judo practice or training. Even when you are not on the mat your fullest energies should be directed to those who are exercising. Good manners are as much a part of Judo as the execution of proper offensive and defensive techniques.

One of the most important ceremonies in Judo is the salutation, or bow. This is not just a greeting; it is a demonstration of your respect for your opponent and should be made seriously before and after all practices and contests.

Upon entering or leaving the Dojo or gymnasium where you practice Judo, you come to a brief halt and perform a Tache-Re. At the edge of the mat, you again bow, facing inward. The Tache-Re is also performed upon leaving the mat and before and after each workout with a partner or opponent.

The Tache-Re is performed while standing about 6 feet from your partner or opponent. In class, or during a workout, it is accomplished by common consent. In a tournament, however, this may be performed at the command "Rei" by the referee.

This is the proper posture for the Tache-Re. Notice the angle of the feet.

You bow from the waist, allowing your arms and hands to slide down and slightly forward. Direct your eyes forward and down.

Performing the Tache-Re

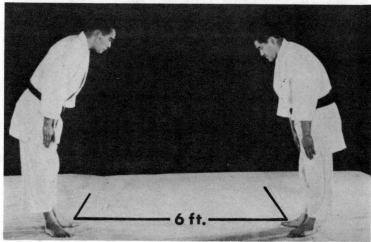

The Zarai, or sitting bow, is performed before and after each class period and Judo tournament. This salutation is done by all of the Judoka simultaneously.

You begin the Zarai from the standing position. Bring your left foot back and kneel, keeping the bottom of your toes on the mat. Your right hand is along your right thigh. Your left knee is in line with your right foot. Head and body are erect, eyes straight ahead.

Now, bring your right leg back, and place it alongside your left leg. Your body is erect, hands touching sides, knees parallel.

Beginning the Zarai

Front view

Knees parallel   *Sit back*   *Front view*

Reverse your feet and toes so that the toe-nails are facing *down*. Place the big toe of your right foot, over the big toe of your left foot. Sit back on your feet.

Bring both hands inward to the front of your thighs. Notice the distance between the knees. Now, without raising up, bow forward to a 45-degree angle. Bend your head down slightly but keep your eyes raised. Bring your hands down on the mat.

Right toe over left   *Side and front view of bow*

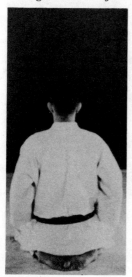

Hold the bow for a two count, then return to the sitting position. You stand up by reversing the same procedure you used to kneel.

The color of the belt worn by a Judoka denotes his rank. There are three ranks—white belt, brown belt and black belt. The black belt is the highest, white the lowest. There are three grades of the brown belt, and ten degrees of the black belt. The sixth, seventh and eighth degree black belt holders may wear a red and white sectioned belt, and the ninth and tenth degrees may wear a *solid* red belt. A Judoka may earn promotions in rank through knowledge, demonstrated ability of various Judo techniques, time in grade and competition in tournaments.

Three different belts

JUDOGI

About to begin

Now that you know something of the history, dress, ceremony and rank of Judo, you are ready to begin practice. Before an actual Judo session, it is necessary to loosen your muscles and joints through a series of exercises.

These warming-up exercises are of vital importance to your own safety on the mat, because you are far less likely to be injured if your body is relaxed and flexible. Repeat each of the following exercises several times before each workout.

First, with your feet about 18 inches apart, swing both arms to the right side and left side. Allow your body to pivot freely on your hips.

Swinging and pivoting

Rolling the head

Swinging the arms up

To loosen your neck muscles, relax and roll your head in complete circles. Keep your eyes open. Alternate directions. Next, rock your head forward and back, then tilt it from side to side. Keep your chin forward and try to touch your ear to your shoulder.

Swinging down

Bending to the side

Swinging in a circle   *Loosening the knees*

Now, with arms extended, swing your hands upward and back, stretching as far as you can. Keep your head back.

Next, swing your arms forward and down so that your arms pass between your legs. Keep both legs straight. Straighten up and repeat the exercise, stretching a little more each time.

With your feet spread 30 inches, and without bending forward, slide one arm down your side to below the knee. At the same time, sweep your other arm upward in a circular motion so that it almost touches your head. You should feel the stretch from your heel along the entire side of your body to your fingertips. Reverse the exercise to the other side.

With feet 30 inches apart, hands raised, palms forward, and legs straight, bring your body and arms down in a circular motion, around the right side of your body. Follow across to the left side. Continue this sweeping motion until your arms are high above your head. As your body straightens up, stretch backwards as far as you can. Reverse the procedure from left to right.

To loosen the knee joints, bend forward (see above), legs straight, feet 18 inches apart. Press backward on both knees with the palms of your hands. Now drop into a squat position.

Squat position

Stretching leg

Keep your heels raised, knees pointed outward, and buttocks as low as possible.

To stretch your leg muscles, stand with your feet 30 inches apart, and parallel to each other. Bend one leg, knee pointed forward, and lower your body to a squat position with the weight centered over the heel of your bent leg. Simultaneously, *raise* the toes of your other foot, so that only the heel is in contact with the mat. Keep your leg straight and press on the thigh just above the knee. Without moving your feet from their position on the mat, stand up and reverse the action by bending your *other* knee forward.

For the next exercise, sit on the mat and grasp one leg just above the ankle. With your other hand, revolve your foot with a cranking motion to the right and to the left. Bend your foot forward and backward, and from side to side. Rub your feet briskly with both hands. Now shake your wrists vigorously and pop your knuckles.

Loosening the ankle

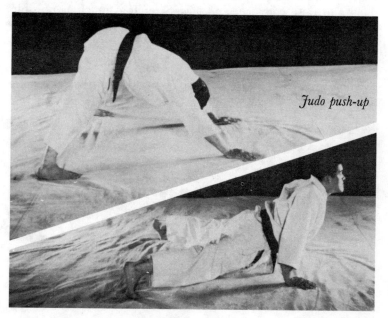

Stretching backs of legs

From a sitting position, spread your legs as far as possible. Reach forward and try to touch the mat with your forehead. Sit up and repeat the exercise. From the same position, touch each knee with your forehead several times.

Next, try several Judo push-ups. With your feet set wide apart, hands on mat at shoulder width, push *back* as far as possible. Lower your chin close to the mat and *arch* your head and body downward and forward, then up, until your body is supported by your toes and hands. Your chest and waist should follow the swooping arc of your head. Return to the first position by pushing up and back.

Judo push-up

Touching toes

Rocking on the back

In the sitting position with legs extended, reach forward and try to touch your toes or beyond them.

Next, bring your arms and legs up and over your head to the rear. The backs of your hands and big toes should touch the mat. Return to the sitting position and touch your toes.

Lie on your stomach and place your hands in the small of your back. Alternately raise your head and chest, then lower them and raise your feet and legs. Stretch as much as possible each time. Then, raise both head *and* legs and rock back and forth.

Rocking on the front

A push-up with a twist

Now, assume the position for a push-up. Bring your right leg under your left leg as far as possible, twisting your body to the right. Repeat the exercise to the left, concentrating on hip action.

Lie on your back, lift your head, raise your arms, and clench your fists. Bring your right knee back to your chest and *snap* your left leg forward. Keep your toes curled back. Reverse legs and repeat the exercise.

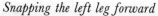

Snapping the left leg forward

The body bridge

The next exercise is the body bridge. Lie on your back and bring your arms up and back over your head so they are parallel to the mat. Bring your feet back as far under your buttocks as possible. Roll your head back and arch your body up, so that only your head and toes touch the mat. Keep your chin tilted up. Return to the first position by rolling your head forward and lowering your body.

This is similar to the body bridge. Assume the first position. As you bridge upwards, roll your head back and to the right. Twist your right hip and shoulder down. Swing your left arm up and to the right. Roll your head and body back to the starting position and repeat the exercise on the other side.

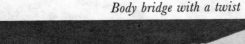

Body bridge with a twist

The back snake crawl

This mat exercise is called the back snake crawl. Lie on the mat, face up, arms close to your body, elbows at your hips. Pull your left leg back and bring your left foot close to your left hip. Push with this foot and scoot the body backwards. At the same time, twist onto your right side and bring your left arm across your head. Now, twist to the left side and repeat the exercise until you have moved 15 or 20 feet across the mat.

You will have to study and work hard before you have mastered these techniques, but the thrill of winning a Judo tournament is worth every minute of the work and practice.

2. Breakfalls

HON-SHIZENTAI

Beginning Judo requires a thorough knowledge of how to stand. Here is a Judoka, or Judo contestant, standing in the correct natural posture or Hon-Shizentai. Notice the relaxed, "comfortable" stance. The weight is evenly distributed—feet parallel about shoulder-width apart. Body erect. Knees relaxed. Eyes level.

This is known as the right, natural posture or Migi-Shizentai. In this traditional Judo stance the right foot is extended slightly forward. The weight of the body is adjusted accordingly, to maintain equal distribution and balance.

This is Hidari-Shizentai—the left natural posture, which is the Judo stance with the left foot forward.

HON-SHIZENTAI

MIGI — SHIZENTAI

HIDARI — SHIZENTAI

These then are the three basic Judo stances, known as "natural" postures: Hon-Shizentai, Migi-Shizentai and Hidari-Shizentai. Natural . . . right . . . and left.

While there are various places to grasp an opponent's jacket or Judogi during a Judo match, this is the basic grip.

The right hand clasps the opponent's lapel at the height of the armpit, while the other hand seeks and holds the sleeve just

Grasping opponent's jacket

below the bend of the elbow. This is the basic hold from the right natural posture. Because both men are employing the same hold—this view serves to illustrate the position of both hands.

The same basic hold from a left natural position calls for a reversal of hand positions as you see here.

Grasping with left hand

Moving forward

At all times during the course of a Judo match, or practice, the primary objective is to maintain balance and proper control of the body. In a hand-to-hand bout you must be ready to act instantaneously with perfect freedom. Therefore, when moving on a Judo mat, you must always strive to maintain a firm balance base. This is accomplished by moving forward in the manner you see here. One foot is advanced—the other is brought quickly up. Then the starting foot is moved forward again. The feet never pass each other as in ordinary walking. This rule applies to starts with either foot, and the same practice is religiously followed in retreating.

Moving sideways

In moving sideways, the same general principle holds true. The trained Judo player moves one foot out—the other follows just far enough to establish a balanced base. Then the starting foot is advanced again. The feet are never crossed, or brought too close together because these actions leave you momentarily awkward and vulnerable.

In turning right or left—whichever the case may be—the lead foot is advanced in a circular movement, while the ball of the other foot forms a firm pivot. In Judo, turns are known as

Tai-Sabaki and are widely employed in throwing an opponent in a manner like this:

Notice here how a turn to the left utilizes the whole body in the starting of a throw.

Just as the aim in a Judo match is to maintain balance and control of yourself at all times, one of the goals of offensive action is to upset the balance of your opponent. Breaking the posture of your opponent is known as Kuzushi.

O = Opponent

Beginning the throw

KUZUSHI

There are many ways of breaking your opponent's balance
in Judo. In the upper left hand corner a pushing technique is
used to break balance to the direct rear. In the upper right
hand corner a sudden pull is used to break balance to the front
corner. In the center, the opponent's balance is weakened by
lifting or floating him to his toes. The bottom two scenes
illustrate the upsetting of the balance to the left and to the
right. Upsetting your opponent's balance makes it easier to
execute the technique you have in mind—even when facing
a stronger opponent—because loss of balance means loss of
strength.

However, to take a closer look, the initial maneuvering for balance does not mean just pushing, or pulling, or lifting. Sometimes you "push" and then stop. Pull and suddenly loosen. Pull and then push. Push or pull from left to right with quick reverses. A skilful series of feints and pressures breaks your opponent's balance. These methods of Kuzushi are vital to "setting up" the opponent for the continuation of your attack.

Maneuvering the opponent

Before we get into the area of Judo techniques, however, proper caution and instruction demand that a study be made of Ukemi, the Judo art of breaking the fall. Ukemi enables a

UKEMI

Falling without harm

Judoka to fall safely and easily. On the mat, Ukemi enables you to land without shock or injury when being thrown. It's also invaluable in lessening the effects of accidental falls in everyday life.

Ukemi is important to all the techniques of Judo, including the art of throwing. It is rightly said that the best way to learn to throw an opponent is to *be thrown* ten thousand times. Learning to break the fall effectively requires proper conditioning and perfecting of timing. Therefore, Ukemi training must begin with a series of simple exercises:

Step 1

From a prone position—head and shoulders lifted as much as possible, eyes directed toward the knot on the belt—raise your arms vertically to a position like the above (Step 1).

Step 2

Then, freely slap the mat with both hands and under forearms, bouncing them off the mat and directly up again (Step 2). This practice should be started slowly and cautiously. Gradually increase the tempo as your conditioning improves until you are striking the mat quite quickly and sharply.

Looking at the beginning exercise from a side perspective, direct your attention to the position of the head. It never

Side view

touches the floor. One of the main purposes of the breakfall is to keep your head from striking the mat. Therefore, throughout the course of these exercises it is vitally important that you keep your eyes fixed on the knot of your belt.

This is a sequence demonstrating side-to-side body rolling. Lying on your back, raise your head, shoulders and legs off the mat. Bring your right arm up and away from your body, palm outward (Step 1).

Roll over on your right side bringing both legs and your right arm down together, striking the mat as a single unit (Step 2). The outer edge of your right foot, the inner edge of your left foot, and the striking arm all break the fall simultaneously. At

Step 1   Step 2

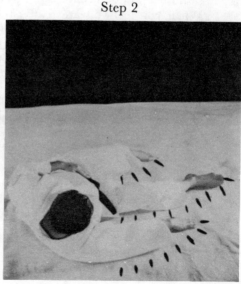

Roll to the side

the conclusion of the roll, both feet should be parallel and about waist width apart.

Without hesitation bring both feet up in a high arc and repeat the roll to the other side: one continuous action from side-to-side, without stopping. NOTE: Head and upper neck are off the mat at all times.

When you feel you are ready, the falling practice may be started from a sitting position. With legs extended, raise your arms to the front bringing them simultaneously over your head (Step 1). Then topple over backwards swinging your legs up in a generous arc (Step 2). Bring your arms downward in the

Step 1

Step 2

Side view

slapping motion learned, timing the action to beat the mat just at the moment your upper back makes contact.

At the end of the sequence note that your head and shoulders never touch the mat. Chin should be kept on your chest and your eyes should be trained on the knot on your belt. The action is continuous—at the completion of the backfall, you return without pause to a sitting position and then the backfall is repeated.

Ukemi from a squat

After you have mastered Ukemi from a sitting position you may advance to practicing the fall from a squat.

Step 1

Step 2

Step 3

This is the sequence of action. With arms extended, fingers slightly overlapping, buttocks resting on your raised heels (Step 1), roll over backwards, raising your arms overhead (Step 2). Again, as your back makes contact, your arms should be brought down with a slicing motion to strike the mat just as your back makes contact (Step 3).

Then bring your arms up with a snap, and return to a squat position in one continuous motion (Step 4). In falling, remember to keep your buttocks close to your heels and *your head and neck up off the mat*.

Step 4

| Step 1 | Step 2 | Step 3 |

This is the sequence of the backfall from a standing position. With arms parallel to the floor (Step 1), start dropping your body by bending your knees and raising your toes. As you are lowering, raise your arms high (Step 2). Tuck your heels in close to your buttocks as in the fall from a squat (Step 3).

At the moment your balance is lost, your arms should be brought down sharply to strike the mat at the same time as your back makes contact (Step 4). Legs should be brought up and over in the follow-through. Chin tucked in. Head and neck off the mat. Keep your eyes focused on the knot on your belt. Allow your arms to snap up and off the mat at the finish of the arm beat. Rise and repeat.

Step 4

Step 1

Step 2

This is the beginning position (Step 1) for a sidefall from a sitting posture. Your legs are outstretched to the front, one hand resting easily and naturally on your thigh. Your striking arm is held across your chest in the manner illustrated.

Then roll to the striking hand side, raising the legs (Step 2), while at the same time striking the mat to break the fall. Keep your head and shoulders up off the mat. Allow the striking arm to bounce up after the blow. Arm and hand should be relaxed throughout the exercise. After completing the fall, allow your legs to drop and, sitting up, repeat the fall to the other side. Continue to alternate sides during the conditioning period.

410

Sidefalls from a squatting posture begin like this (Step 1). With your striking arm in cross-chest position, turn your opposite knee somewhat out (Step 2), and the leg on the falling side out to the front and across the body in the direction away from the fall.

Fall to your side, striking the mat with your arm and hand to break the fall (Step 3). Your body should land with your head and neck off the mat, your chin tucked in. Your legs are allowed to come up and follow through. Rising to a squat position, continue the exercise by practicing falls to either side, alternately.

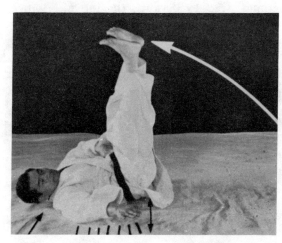

Step 3

The sideways breakfall from a standing position is similar to the squat, but from a higher level, both feet parallel. Bring your right arm downward and across your body to the left side (Step 1). At the same time throw your leg in a sweeping motion across your body. Bend your left knee deeply to lower your body. The hip should touch the heel as you roll.

Then bring your arm down hard, breaking the fall by striking the mat with your entire arm—from armpit to fingertips (Step 2). Allow the legs to come up in a follow-through. Rise and repeat to the left side.

You will sometimes need to perform the forward somersault: From a standing position advance your right foot one

Step 2

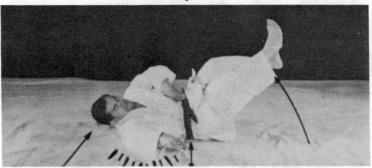

412

pace forward. Lower your body and place your left hand parallel with your right foot and in line with your rear foot to form a triangle (Step 1). Note the position of the fingers on the left hand—they point inward directly towards your right foot.

Step 1

Next, place your right hand on the mat, palm down, fingers pointing to the left foot (Step 2).

Step 2

Tuck your head in, turning your chin to the left. Using the rounded right arm as the outer edge of a wheel, roll over the arm and over the right shoulder (Step 3).

Step 3

Step 4

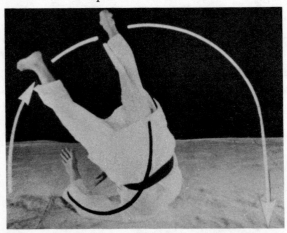

Bring both feet over in a big arc, rolling on an imaginary angle of a line running from your right shoulder to your left leg (Step 4). At no time does your head come in contact with the mat.

Just before the upper left of your body strikes the mat, slap the mat with your left arm to break the roll (Step 5). At the conclusion, your head and shoulders should be up off the mat—feet parallel. Practice this exercise by alternating left and right feet and hand positions.

Step 5

The next rolling breakfall is the one-hand forward somersault. This is the same as the two-hand forward maneuver from a higher level, the left hand kept free from the mat. Again, as you follow this sequence, note the head and neck are kept up off the mat.

One-hand somersault

Diving breakfall

After you have mastered the one- and two-hand forward somersaults you continue to the diving breakfall: Take 6 or 8 running steps and dive in a running somersault over a fellow Judoka. As you become more proficient, add other kneeling figures to lengthen your dive.

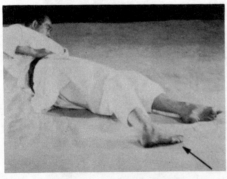

Ending in reclining position

All of the somersaulting breakfalls should be practiced in two different ways: (1) Ending in a reclining position and (2) allowing the momentum of your roll to carry you completely over and back to a standing position.

In falling forward from a kneeling position extend your arms horizontally (Step 1),

Step 1

and fall forward on your hands, fingers turned slightly inward (Step 2).

Step 2

Just before your chest contacts the mat, turn your head sideways, so that it is parallel to the mat and not touching (Step 3).

Step 3

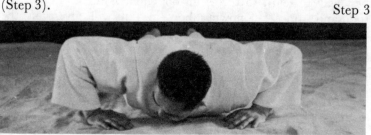

Falling forward from a standing position is much the same as from a kneeling position—make contact with the mat in the same manner. At the moment of contact with the mat only your hands and your toes touch the mat. Do not allow your knees or chest to touch until after contact has been made.

Beginning position

The fall

Learning to fall properly is a Judo *must*. Remember, "The best way to learn to throw an opponent is to be thrown ten thousand times." Knowing how to fall will give you the confidence you need to perform naturally—at your best—and truly enjoy "the gentle art."

418

3. The Art of Throwing

After learning to prepare and condition yourself for the vigorous sport of Judo, the next concern is Tachi-Waza or the art of throwing from a standing position. Tachi-Waza is divided into three categories: Te-Waza, or hand techniques, in

"O" identifies opponent

which the opponent is thrown mainly through the action of the thrower's hands (or the hands play a major role in the throwing), Koshi-Waza or hip techniques, in which hip action is the main feature of the throwing, and Ashi-Waza, *the leg and foot tech-*

ASHI-WAZA

niques. (While the word "Ashi" in Japanese, literally means "foot," in Judo usage Ashi techniques include the entire leg from just above the knee as well.)

The leg and foot techniques are the dramatic Judo throws by which a small man is able to toss a much larger opponent with only a slight movement of the foot. They are said to be the essence of Judo technique. Ashi-Waza is the most scientific of the three general techniques and therefore requires deftness and precision timing which can come only from diligent practice.

One Judoka throws another

Step 1   Step 2

From a right natural posture we are going to describe De-Ashi-Harai, an advancing foot sweep, leg technique. Holding your Judo partner's lapel with your right hand, and his outer, middle sleeve with your left hand (Step 1), withdraw your right foot to your right back corner making your opponent advance his left foot.

At the same time, with your left hand pull on your opponent's right sleeve forcing him to advance his right foot in order to maintain balance (Step 2).

At the precise instant his foot is about to touch the mat, turn your left foot (Step 3) and apply the sole against your op-

O = Opponent

Step 3

ponent's outside ankle and right heel. Sweep his leg out from under him in a forward and inward direction (Step 4). At the same time, pull his right sleeve strongly down, completing the throw (Step 5).

Step 4

Step 5

Step 1

This is Hiza-Guruma, the knee wheel, to your opponent's right leg. From a right natural posture, bring your right foot back and to the right a half-step, turning your foot so that it faces your opponent's right heel (Step 1). At the same time lift upward on his lapel and pull on his right arm, breaking his balance to the right front corner. Then pull his left sleeve in an upward motion floating him on his left foot. Push up with your right hand; simultaneously bring your left leg up, knee straight, and gently place the sole of your foot against the outside front of his knee (Step 2).

Notice from the close-up photo that care should be taken, at time of contact, to *gently* place the sole of the foot against the knee. This is not a kicking or striking motion, which might injure your opponent—but a blocking action.

424

Step 2

Pivoting on your right foot as much as possible, and continuing the twisting motion, throw your opponent over the blocking foot (Step 3).

Step 3

Step 1

The next throw is a knee wheel (Hiza-Guruma), too,
applied to the leg in the right back corner. Starting from a
right, natural posture, step back a full pace to your right rear,
pulling slightly on your partner's left lapel, but loosely holding
his right sleeve. This will cause him to take a step forward with his
left foot (Step 1). Then relax the forward pull of your right
hand, and suddenly reverse your pressure to a solid push
against his left shoulder—pushing it back and around to the
right rear, while, at the same time, pulling on the left sleeve to
create a circular "steering" motion (Step 2). This will break his
balance to the right front corner.

Bring your left leg up now (Step 3) and place the sole of
your left foot, leg straight, on the side of his knee in a holding
action.

Your opponent is thrown over your foot with an unbroken
continuation of the steering motion (Steps 4 and 5).

0 = Opponent

Step 2

Step 3

Steps 4 and 5

Step 1

Now we turn to the hip techniques. This is the beginning of Uki-Goshi—the floating hip throw. Starting in a right, natural position (Step 1), step back one pace—while pulling and lifting your opponent with your right hand on his left lapel, causing him to advance his left foot (Step 2). Then with your left hand, pull him slightly upward to make him float and break balance towards his right front corner.

Next, encircle his waist with your right arm and at the same time turn (Step 3), placing your right foot inside his right foot and moving your left foot back around in front and outside of his right foot—pulling him up snug.

Notice that your back must be kept straight. Solid contact must be maintained from hip to armpit by keeping erect and not leaning forward.

Throw him (Steps 4 and 5), twisting your hips from right to left.

428

Step 2

Step 3

Steps 4 and 5

O-GOSHI

Step 1

Step 2

To execute O-Goshi—the major loin throw—start from a right, natural position. Follow up by moving your left foot back one step (Step 1), forcing your opponent to advance his right foot to maintain balance; then, with your right hand, pull on his lapel, forcing him to bring his left foot parallel to his right. At this point, lift with both hands, floating him to his toes, breaking his balance to the direct front (Step 2).

Then, use your right arm to encircle his waist. Turn, placing both feet inside his (Step 3). Make solid contact with your right side from hip to shoulder. Bend your knees to bring your

O = Opponent

Step 3

Step 4

hip line below his belt. Straighten your knees—and with a twist of your hips from right to left, throw your opponent over your hip (Step 4).

Complete the throw (Step 5).

Step 5

Step 1

Another foot technique, O-Soto-Gari—or major outer reaping—is one of the most popular contest throws. It starts from the right natural posture (Step 1).

Make your opponent step forward on his right foot by pulling him gently to his right front corner. Move your left foot to a point a little outside his right foot, and break his balance to the right rear corner by the combined action of both hands. Your left hand pulls in (Step 2), and your right hand pushes up and back (Step 3, a view from the other side). Notice the vertical position of the hand so that your forearm will come in contact with his chest.

With his balance broken in the right back corner (notice in Step 4 that his left foot is on his toes and all of his balance

Step 2   Step 3

rests on his right foot), raise your *right* leg and swing it forward
and past his right leg. Then, suddenly "reap" or sweep back-

Step 4

Step 5

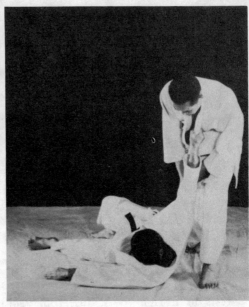

Step 6

wards and outwards near the middle of his right back outer thigh, making contact with the same region of your right thigh (Step 5). At the same time push with your right forearm, and your opponent will fall backwards. He will be thrown as in Step 6.

The next throw to be demonstrated is Sasai-Tsurikomi-Ashi, or propping-drawing-ankle throw. Beginning from a right, natural posture, advance with your left foot, and push with your left arm, forcing your opponent to step back on his right foot (Step 1).

"O" identifies opponent

SASAI-TSURIKOMI-ASHI

Step 1

By lifting and pulling with your right hand and at the same time pulling with your left hand, break his balance towards his right front corner (Step 2). Seize that moment to place the sole of your left foot against the lower part of his right leg

Step 2

Step 3

(Step 3). Simultaneously twist your body back and around to the left, pulling hard with your left hand on his right sleeve and pushing with your right hand on his left lapel (Step 4). He loses his balance and is thrown over your propping foot to his left side as in Step 5.

Step 4

Step 5

O-UCHI-GARI

Step 1

In performing O-Uchi-Gari, the major inner reaping, you first pull your opponent to the left front corner (Step 1).

You break his balance to the left rear corner and swiftly place the back of your right knee to the back of the knee of your opponent's extended left leg (toes pointed downward as in Step 2). Then reap it towards your right back corner, describing a big arc with your toes (Step 3).

Step 2

Step 3

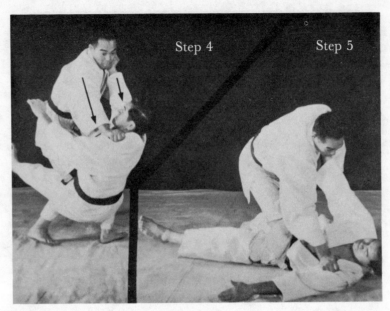

The fall is completed by pushing directly downward with both of your hands (Steps 4 and 5). All these movements are simultaneous, and co-ordinated. If properly executed, your opponent will fall directly backwards.

IPPON-
SEOI-
NAGE

Step 1

In Ippon-Seoi-Nage, the one-hand-over-the-shoulder throw from the right natural posture, step back one-half pace with your left foot. At the same time, draw your opponent forward and slightly up, causing his balance to be broken to the right front corner (Step 1).

Then, step *across* with your right foot, placing it just in front of his right foot. Then, bending your knees slightly and pivoting on the ball of your right foot, move your left foot back inside his left foot and hook your right elbow up under his right armpit (Step 2). Keep your back in close contact with his chest and abdomen, as you see in Step 3. Straighten your legs, bend your body forward and pull both arms downward.

Step 2

Step 3

O = Opponent

Step 4

Throw your opponent over your right shoulder, as shown in Step 4. The essence of Kodokan Judo lies in the refinement of throwing techniques. The beginning throws you have seen demonstrated are an introduction to the simple, scientific logic that forms the base for your entire Judo training. Learn them well because you will use them over and over again.

4. Additional Throwing Techniques

Step 1   Step 2

Because the throwing techniques represent the greater part of the abilities of a Judo player we shall continue the demonstration of throws in this unit, starting with Marote-Seoi-Nage, the two-arm shoulder throw. Step back on your left foot (Step 1) and pull your opponent's upper body forward (Step 2). The moment his balance is broken to the right front corner, or directly forward as you see in Step 2, advance your right foot to the inner side of his right foot.

441

Then pivot on the ball of your right foot, and place your left foot inside your opponent's left foot, as you see in Step 3a. Note: Your back and hip make a solid contact from his upper chest down to his thigh. It's important that your hip be snug to his thigh.

Step 3a

Step 3b

From a front perspective (Step 3b) notice your body must be perfectly parallel, directly in line with your opponent. Your right arm is bent at the elbow and under his right armpit—

O = Opponent

wrist locked forward. At this moment he is floating on his toes, while you are in a low posture, below his center of gravity.

Step 4

Step 5

Suddenly you straighten your knees, raise your loins, lean your upper body forward and throw him to the front over your right shoulder, completing the throw as you can see in Steps 4 and 5.

Step 1

This is Ko-Soto-Gari, the minor outside reap. Starting from a right natural position, pull lightly to the front with both hands—your opponent will pull back to retain his balance (Step 1).

Taking full advantage of his backward reaction, provide an additional force of your own in the form of a steering action with both hands, which shifts his balance to his heels, and his right back corner. You step to his right side (Step 2) and in one continuous motion you pull down with your left hand, push up and back with your right hand, and reap his right leg from under him with your left foot (Step 3a).

In a close-up of the action from the other side (Step 3b), notice the position of your foot at the exact moment of contact during the reap. Your reaping leg should be absolutely straight, and your foot turned to apply the sole flat against your op-

Step 2

Step 3a

Step 3b

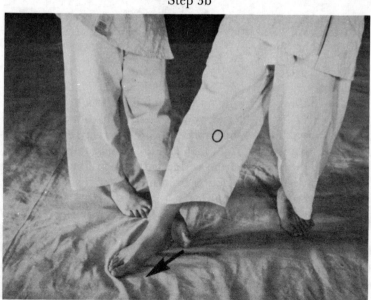

445

ponent's heel. Follow through in the direction shown. He will go down directly at your feet, as shown in Steps 4 and 5.

Step 4

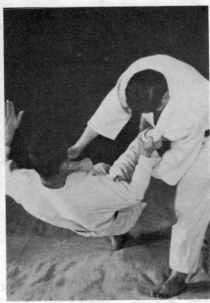

Step 5

Now, Ko-Uchi-Gari, the minor inside reap. From a right natural start, bring your left foot back and around as you see here. By pulling naturally on your opponent's right sleeve, and pushing his left shoulder down and back with your right hand, you will break his balance to the back left corner (Step 1).

As he advances his right foot slightly to maintain his stance, reap his right front leg from within with your right foot. Step 2 shows a close-up of the action from in front of his left leg. Pay particular attention to your leg, extended straight, and the way your foot, sole forward, cups and sweeps his right heel straight ahead in the direction of his toes.

O = Opponent

KO-UCHI-GARI

Step 1

Keeping your eyes directed towards the back of your right hand, press downward and back with that hand and forearm while your left hand pulls on his left sleeve. He will go down in his right back corner, as shown in Step 3.

Step 2

Step 3

The lift-pull-hip-throw

This is Tsuri-Komi-Goshi, the lift-pull-hip-throw. The first two words, Tsuri-Komi, refer to the beginning lift-pull action. The mastering of the lift-pull is important because it is a basic beginning for many of the popular contest throws. Goshi means hip. So this is the *lift-pull* action as it's used to set up *a hip throw*.

Begin stepping back with your left foot, while pulling up and forward on his right sleeve. Lift upward and forward on his left lapel and float him up, making him vulnerable on his toes (Step 1).

Pivoting on your right foot, with knees slightly bent, you swing around and place your left foot within his left foot. Draw him up snugly to your back with right elbow under his left armpit, body low, hip against his right thigh (Step 2a).

Step 1   Step 2a

In the front view of the position before the throw (Step 2b),
note the firm grasp of your right hand on his left lapel, your

Step 2b

Step 3

left hand on your opponent's right sleeve. As he leans over your back, lift with your hips. As you straighten your knees you will push his thighs upward. Follow by twisting your body to the left, giving a pull with both hands. Your opponent will revolve over your hip (Step 3) and be thrown.

SODI-TSURI-KOMI-GOSHI

This is Sodi-Tsuri-Komi-Goshi, the sleeve-lifting-pull-hip throw. This hip throw is essentially the same as the hip technique you have just seen. The difference? For greater leverage the lifting is applied to the sleeve rather than the lapel.

Start by switching your right hand from your foe's lapel to his left sleeve. Gripping his sleeve near the top of the elbow, slide your right foot near your left heel, and draw your opponent forward by pulling on his left sleeve (Step 1). Now step across with your left foot toward his left toes, with your knees bent. At the same time push his right arm straight upward (Step 2). The combined action of lifting his right sleeve and pulling on his left sleeve will float him to his toes.

Step 1

Step 2

"O" identifies opponent

Step 3

Step 4

Next, slide your right foot to the front of his right foot and complete the clockwise turning of your body, forming a solid chest and back contact diagonally down his body from armpit to left forethigh (Step 3). By lifting your opponent with your legs and hip, and turning your body from left to right in coordination with the movements of your hands, you complete the throw (Step 4).

OKURI-ASHI-HARAI

Okuri-Ashi-Harai, the sweeping ankle throw, is usually applied when the opponent is moving to the side. Starting from the right natural position as your opponent moves to his left, move in rhythm with him.

Step 1a

As he steps out to the left and widens his stance, before he can close the gap by following with his right foot, press his right elbow against his right side with your left hand. At the same time push—then pull—with your lapel hand to float him on the toes of his right foot (Steps 1a and b).

453

Step 1b

At that very moment, with your left leg well extended, sweep his right foot toward his left in much the same manner as the advancing foot sweep (Step 2). Following through with a counter-clockwise movement of your hands, sweep your foot

Step 2

Step 3

across and well beyond your right leg, throwing your opponent as shown in Step 3.

Step 1

This is the Tai-Otoshi, the body drop. It is a hand technique. From a right natural posture bring your left foot back and around in a semi-circle, simultaneously pulling on his sleeve in a wide arc. Your right foot remains pointing toward your opponent (Step 1).

Use both hands as though they were turning a steering wheel—pull with your left hand and forearm! Pushing with your right hand, palm down against his chest, wheel him

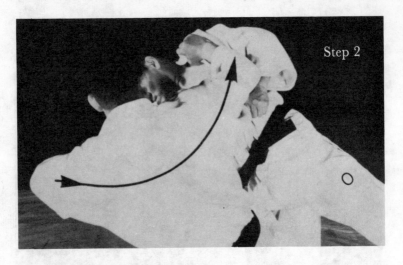

(Step 2) and thus break his balance to his right front corner (Step 3).

Step 3

Then, pivoting on the ball of your left foot, swing around as shown in Step 4. Place your right foot past his right ankle in a blocking action with both knees bent.

456

Step 4

Straightening your right leg with a snap (demonstrated in the upper left hand corner of Step 5) apply both your hands and body in a quick, twisting motion—throwing him over your blocking leg in a manner like this. (Note that his left arm, raised high, is in a perfect position to break his fall.)

Step 5

Step 1

The next technique we will cover is Harai-Goshi, the sweeping loin throw. In the usual start from the right natural posture, step back half a pace with your left foot and turn your right side to your opponent's direct front, at the same time exerting a forward and upward pull on his right sleeve. Meanwhile your right hand lifts and pushes in the same direction, lifting him to his toes and breaking his balance in the right front corner (Step 1).

Now, as you pivot on the sole of your right foot, bring your left foot back and around parallel to your right foot—in between and in front of your opponent's stance (Step 2). Your back turns to his front and you insert your right elbow and forearm under his armpit (Step 3).

Step 2

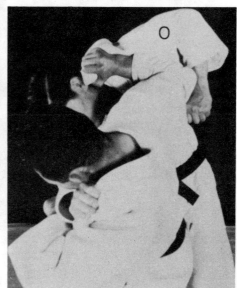

Step 3

Now, maintain solid leg contact between your own body and his front, from armpit to hip, and apply the back of your thigh—from calf to hip—to the front and outer side of his leg and thigh, with your toes pointed down and curled, leg straight (Step 4).

Step 4

Step 5   Step 6

By sweeping around, pushing with your right hand and pulling with your left, you will throw your opponent dramatically over your sweeping leg (Steps 5 and 6).

Uchi-Mata, the inner thigh throw, is the No. 1 contest throw. Move your right foot to a position where it points across the front of your opponent's toes, and at the same time lift upward with both hands. You will float him out of balance, as shown in Step 1.

As you pivot on your right foot, quickly skip your left foot back to the position you see here. Then with one continuous motion you swing your right leg between his legs (Step 2).

0 = Opponent

Step 1

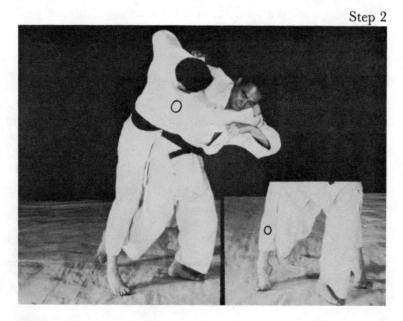

461

Step 3

Now reap his left inner thigh with the back of your right thigh (Step 3). With a simultaneous wheeling action of your hands, toss him over your loin (Step 4).

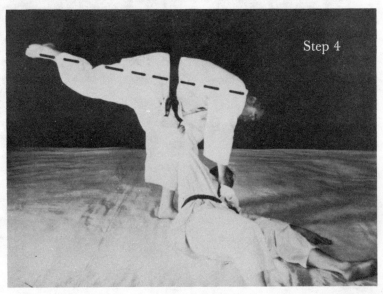

Step 4

In the same way that a boxer shadow-boxes to improve his footwork and timing, a Judo player practices throwing without a partner. It's called Tandoku-Renshu, self-practice. Here we see the self-practice movements for Marote Seinage, the shoulder throw.

From an imaginary grasping of an opponent in the right natural posture, advance your right leg, knee bent, to the spot where your opponent's right foot would be. Then, pulling with your left hand and lifting with your right, pivot on the sole of your right foot—making a 180-degree turn (Steps 1 and 2).

Step 1

Step 2

Step 3

Step 4

464

Bring your left foot back parallel to your right foot with both knees bent (Step 3). At this precise moment suddenly straighten your knees, come up on your toes, bend your upper body forward and bring your hands and arms down in a pantomime of an actual throw (Step 4). The whole movement should be free flowing and continuous. You repeat this practice, changing to the left natural posture. Similar self-practice exercises can be used to perfect all of the Judo techniques.

This concludes the demonstration of throwing techniques. These beginning throws were selected from each of the many throwing methods existing. They are the introductory throws recommended by the Kodokan school in Tokyo. We confined ourselves solely to illustrating the various throws from the right natural posture, because after you have mastered the throws from the right side you will experience no great difficulty in applying the same methods to a left-hand start. Work hard to refine your throwing techniques—they will serve you well in your Judo days to come.

A quick throw

5. Mat Techniques

KESA-GATAME

Step 1

In order to be a complete Judoka, you must learn how to handle yourself well on the mat. Judo experts say, "40 per cent of a player's training time should be devoted to the refinement of mat techniques." This is a study of these techniques, which are holds and escapes. The first technique we will demonstrate is Kesa-Gatame (scarf hold or lock). Approach your opponent by dropping to one knee, close to his chest, as shown in Step 1.

Then grasp his right arm at the elbow, drawing his arm deeply under your left armpit, as Step 2 illustrates from the side and the front. This gives you strong control of your opponent's right arm.

Now slide your right hand around his neck, and with your

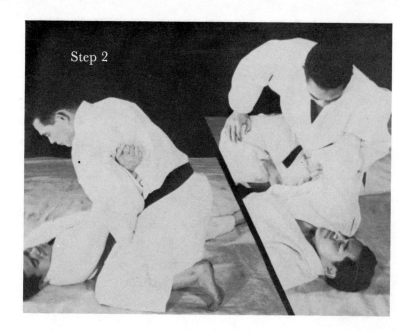

Step 2

right hand grasp the back of his collar with your thumb inside. With your entire right side pressing tightly against his chest, keep your right leg bent and your thigh tight against his arm and shoulder. Extend your left leg behind you to create a firm base (Step 3). Keeping your chin in, lower your head until it

Step 3

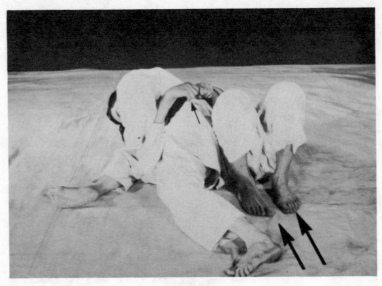

Step 1

touches your opponent's cheek and hold him down, thus
gaining complete control of the upper quarter of his body.

For every holding action in Judo there are one or more
escape techniques. This is one of the most common escapes
from the scarf hold you have just seen. Reach around and grasp
the holder's belt with both hands, and at the same time bring
your heels close to the rear of your own hips (Step 1).

Bring yourself up on your head and toes (Step 2 shows front
and rear views). By twisting your body to your left you will lift
and turn him in a large circle, rolling him over your body.

Another escape from the scarf hold begins the same way.
Grasp your foe's belt with both hands and at the same time
bring your heels in close to your hips, as you did in the first
escape. Next, start to bring yourself up by bridging—creating
space between yourself and the mat. Quickly twisting your
body clockwise, free your right arm and wriggle out on your
knees and stomach (Steps 1 and 2).

Step 2

Steps 1 and 2

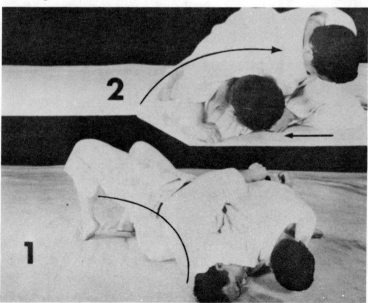

In a third escape from the scarf hold, after you bring yourself up and twist your body to the right, free your right arm and shoulder from his grip. Force your right knee underneath your competitor's body (Step 1).

Step 1

Immediately wrap his left leg with both of your legs (Step 2).

Step 2

Twisting to the left, turn him over on his left side, freeing yourself (Step 3).

Step 3

One of the best opportunities to escape from Kesa-Gatame occurs at the very beginning of the hold. Before your opponent can completely control your right shoulder—quickly grab his right arm by the elbow with your left hand and slip it past your head. This enables you to turn clockwise to your stomach to escape.

Grab his elbow   *Turn clockwise*

Kuzure-Kesa-Gatame is the modified scarf hold. Hold your opponent's right arm firmly under your left armpit. The upper side of his body is held under the right side of your chest, and your right leg is held tight against his body. Your left leg is

KUZURE-KESA-GATAME

extended back and bent at the knee. Lower your head until it presses against his cheek, holding him down.

To escape this hold when it is being applied to you, transfer your body position to the far left of your opponent, then raise both legs high in the direction of his head. At the same time, place your left arm in front of his neck (Step 1).

Step 1

Then bring your legs quickly downward with a snap so the force of their momentum carries your head and shoulders upward, half-reversing positions with your opponent (Steps 2 and 3).

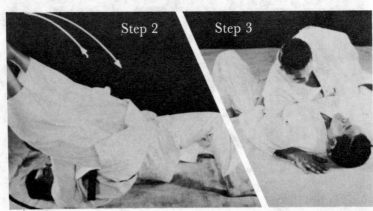

Step 2   Step 3

Step 1

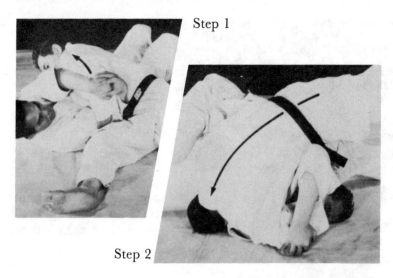

Step 2

An alternative way to escape from this hold is to pull your right arm close to your side. Then reach across with your left hand, locking both hands around his elbow, as shown in Step 1. Pull him up by twisting your body in the direction of his left shoulder, and turn him over (Step 2). Hold him down, as shown in Step 3.

Step 3

KATA-GATAME

The next mat technique is Kata-Gatame, the shoulder lock. As illustrated in Step 1, approach your opponent from his right side. Grasping his right arm with both of yours, raise it and press it against his right cheek (Step 2).

Step 1

Step 2

474

Step 3

Pass your right arm over the tip of his left shoulder and under his neck. With the right side of your neck and shoulder controlling his right arm, pass your left arm over the tip of his left shoulder, and under his neck until both of your hands meet and clasp (Step 3).

From this position, advance your bent, right knee until the knee presses against his right side. Your toes are down and your left leg is extended straight out to your left side to form a rigid triangle (Step 4).

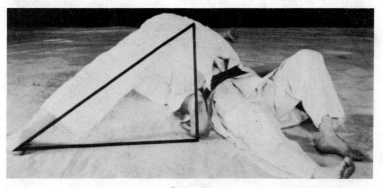

Step 4

Reverse positions and place yourself in the role of the person being held. Here is an escape from the shoulder lock. First,

Step 1

bring your heels close to your hips and bridge upward. At the same time, twist your body to the right to pull your trapped right arm partially out. Then clasp your hands together and push him away to create space (Step 1). Quickly bring your legs over in a somersault and pull your arm out (Step 2).

Step 2

An alternative method of escaping is, after you bridge, to grab his belt with both hands and suddenly twist your body to the left, rolling him over.

An alternate escape

In Kami-Shiho-Gatame, the locking of the upper four quarters, approach your opponent from his head. Then bring your knees up snug to your opponent's shoulders, as shown in Step 1.

Step 1

KAMI-SHIHO-GATAME

Step 2

Step 3

Passing both hands beneath his arms, grasp both sides of his belt with your thumbs turned upward. Turn your head sideways and press it against his stomach (Step 2). Lower your loins so your stomach presses down on his head. Hold him down like this, pinning him from four directions (Step 3).

When the position is reversed and you find yourself in the plight of being held, here is one of the common escapes from the upper-four-quarters lock. Push your opponent upwards by bridging. Then, putting both hands on his upper lapel, push upwards. While your arms are still extended, suddenly lower your body and round your shoulders and back. Bring both knees under his shoulders. By pushing him upward, you will escape to the side.

Step 1

In another escape from the same hold, bring both of your feet close to your hips and raise your body upwards. Place your left hand under your opponent's neck, creating space between your back and the mat (Step 1). As you lower your body, twist

Step 2

your hip to the right side, swinging your left leg over you. Grasp it with both hands (Step 2). Push the holder away with the combined force of your arms and leg, and at the same time, effect your escape by first rolling your body to your right, then quickly in the opposite direction, sliding out on your left side (Step 3).

Step 3

KUZURE-KAMI-SHIHO-GATAME

Step 1

Kuzure-Kami-Shiho-Gatame is the modified locking of the upper four quarters. As your opponent lies on his back, approach and take a position between his right shoulder and head (Step 1).

Bringing both knees in close to his body, slip your right arm under his armpit and grasp the back of his collar, with your four fingers inside and thumb outside (Step 2).

Step 2

Step 3

Pass your left hand under his left shoulder, and grasp the back of his belt with your left hand—thumb inside (Step 3).

Step 4

Close both your arms, straighten your upper body and hold him with your feet spread-eagled to exert counter-pressure in any direction of resistance (Step 4). If the situation warrants, you may also grasp his belt with both hands.

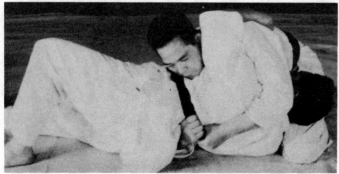

Grasp belt with two hands

481

Step 1

Since Kuzure-Kami-Shiho is a widely used Judo-holding technique, escape knowledge is essential. First, reach over his right shoulder and grab his belt with your left hand. Then apply a series of bridging and bucking actions. After each successive bridge, twist your body to the right—finally pulling your trapped right arm loose! At the same time, work your body up perpendicular to his (Step 1).

After your right arm is free, grasp the front of his belt and push him away, floating his body upward with your left hand (Step 2). As your opponent pushes forward to reconsolidate his position, slide your right knee under his stomach and free yourself by rolling him over on his back. Pull and push in with your hands (Step 3).

Step 2

Step 3

Step 1

In Yoko-Shiho-Gatame—the side-four-quarter hold—approach the side of your opponent (Step 1).

Using both hands, raise your opponent's right arm and place it parallel to your left side (Step 2).

Next, pass your right arm under his left thigh and grasp his belt with your hands—thumb inside—drawing him in (Step 3).

Continuing your hold, slip your left arm under his neck grasping the lapel near his left shoulder with your left hand, encircling his whole body with your arms. With your head

Step 3

484

against his chest, apply even pressure over the entire body area, rendering him immobile (Step 4).

Then draw both legs up as seen here from the rear in Step 5. Your right kneecap presses against his right loin and your left kneecap is pushed up snugly under his right armpit, rendering his right arm and leg useless.

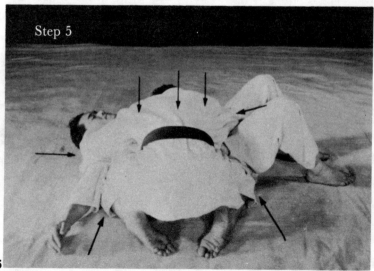

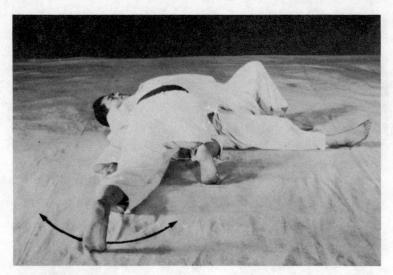

Or you may hold him in this position, with the freedom to extend either leg to counter-escape maneuvers.

When locked in the side-four-quarter hold there are several escape methods you may use. However, you must execute some preliminary maneuvers to create "working room." First, place your left hand on your opponent's collar and grasp his belt near his left hip. Then press down and away with both hands, moving him towards your thigh and sliding upward at the same time (Step 1).

Step 1

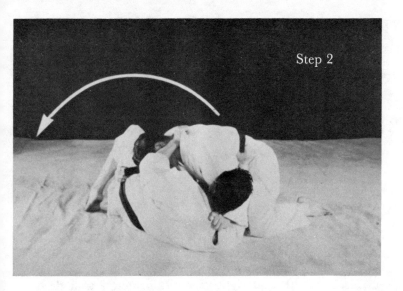

Step 2

Then bridge your body upward and lower your body on your right side, still holding your opponent away. Keep repeating this movement until there is sufficient room to place your right knee under his and roll him over (Step 2).

Or you can bring your right arm under his chest and quickly reverse your direction by twisting to the left to free your right arm from under his left armpit.

Twisting to the left

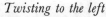

Triangle escape

Another way to escape is to push your opponent down far enough to swing your left leg over his head behind his neck. Apply a scissor with your right knee-pit, forming a triangle to control his head, shoulders and arm.

One of the most popular grappling techniqucs is Kuzure-Yoko-Shiho, the modified lateral locking of four quarters. This pinning principle closely follows Yoko-Shiho, shown previously. The only distinct modification is that the left hand is extended over your opponent's left shoulder, keeping his left arm immobile by locking it securely between your back and left shoulder. Continuing from here, keep your body low, applying even pressure on his chest (Step 1). Then reach under his left

Step 1

KUZURE-YOKO-SHIHO

Step 2

leg with your right hand and grasp the seat of his pants, as shown in Step 2, locking him in from four directions. The position of your legs follows the same pattern as in regular Yoko-Shiho.

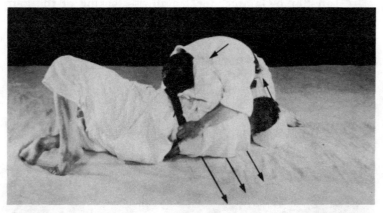

Step 1

Here is a widely used escape method from this hold. Bridge upward with your body, then quickly slide away from him by twisting to your right. At the same time, your right hand pushes against his left hip and your left forearm pushes his head down toward your belt (Step 1).

Step 2

Passing both your hands down through the open space underneath his chest, grab your right foot and push his body upward, stretching your right leg at the same time (Step 2). Complete rolling to the right on your stomach and break his hold.

In Tate-Shiho-Gatame, the lengthwise locking of the four quarters, drop to your left knee to the right side of your

Step 1

TATE-SHIHO-GATAME

Step 2

opponent (Step 1). Then grasp his right arm with both hands and press it down against his cheek (Step 2).

Release your right hand and grasp his left arm, pushing it outward. At the same time straddle his body (Step 3).

Then slide your right arm over his left shoulder and clasp your left hand as shown in Step 4, completely tying up his right arm and shoulder. Bend forward so your neck and right arm

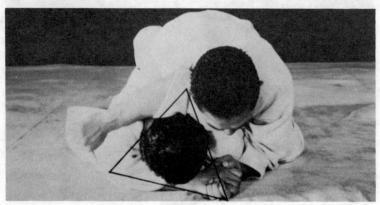

Step 4

form a triangle. Now bring your head down and hold your opponent with the full weight of your body (Step 5).

Step 5

Completed hold

Here is a dramatic view of the completed hold from a rear perspective. Note the position of the feet controlling his hips—an action not visible in the other scenes.

Standard escape

For a standard escape, from the bottom position clasp both hands and force his head downward, breaking his hold on your right shoulder. Then roll to the right to escape.

Step 1

In another escape, grab your opponent's right pant leg at the ankle and pull his leg up, shifting his weight well forward (Step 1).

Then wrap both of your legs around his right leg and turn him over, either to the right or the left, and effect your escape (Step 2).

A point to remember is that you are not a completely trained Judoka until you perfect the mat techniques too. The ability to handle yourself when the action is taken to the mat is an essential part of the mastering of Judo.

Step 2

494

6. Offensive and Defensive Mat Techniques

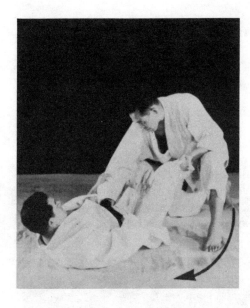

Opponent's defensive position

Offensive mat approaches come into Judo most often as a follow-up after a throw. It is not very difficult to follow up if the opponent is unprepared to take a defensive mat position after he is thrown. However, if he quickly recovers from the throw and takes the proper defensive position—by placing his legs towards you—it is very difficult to continue your attack, unless you know your offensive mat techniques.

The primary obstacle in securing a good pinning hold is penetrating your opponent's defense. To break through his guard and successfully apply your grappling technique, it's

*Breaking through
opponent's defense*

usually necessary to begin with some preliminary maneuvering designed to gain a position for a good pinning hold.

Here is a proper offensive mat posture, as refined by the Kodokan. Your center of gravity is low, yet at the same time you have freedom of mobility in all directions. Your knees are bent, hips down, with your toes on the mat to provide quick change in any direction. For an example of how you continue your offense from this posture, move in and cradle both of his

Offensive mat position

legs firmly in your arms. Then, keeping your body low and
your feet wide apart, push him forward (Step 1).

As he pushes back, suddenly pull back and drop his legs
between your legs. Then slide quickly upwards and hold his
upper body stationary (Step 2).

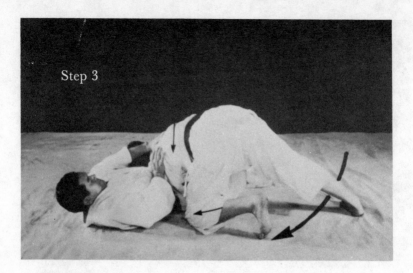

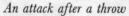

Step 3

Now pivot to your left, and attack his right flank by bringing your left knee against his right arm, securing the side locking of the four quarters (Step 3).

In an attack immediately after a throw, come down to a posture on one knee, grasping his belt with one hand to hold him in position. Then, grasping his pant leg with the other hand, hold his leg where it is while you move around and attack his right flank.

An attack after a throw

Pulling opponent up

In another method, pull your opponent up on his rear haunches and then go in on either side or over his lowered legs.

Still another mat approach is to grasp his pant leg and sleeve, pull him aside and attack his flank. Or move around to attack from his head.

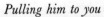

Pulling him to you

Step 1

In a situation where your opponent has been thrown and you remain standing, you may continue your offensive by grasping both of his ankles and sweeping his legs first to his right then back to his left, moving his legs from your approach path (Step 1).

Then quickly step in on his right side, pinning his right hip with your right knee (Step 2) and conclude the hold by pro-

Step 2

Step 1

ceeding to apply Kesa-Gatame or Kata-Gatame. Or, by grasping both pants legs at the knees, press down and to his left (Step 1).

Entering from his right side, immobilize his body with your right knee as you proceed to a pinning technique (Step 2).

Step 2

Grasping opponent's belt

Another way to break through your opponent's defensive posture is to grasp his belt. With your right hand and knee, press down against his inner thigh. Then slide up on his side for a pin hold.

In the shoulder method of approach, split your opponent's legs. Control his right leg by encircling it with your left arm, and then lock it tightly with your arm, shoulder and neck. Press your left shoulder forward towards his chest and at the same time hold his left leg down, with your right hand grasping his trousers (Step 1).

Step 1

Step 2

Then bring your right knee over his left thigh so that your shin presses his thigh down tight to the mat. Now, moving your right hand up from his leg, grasp his left sleeve near the elbow and pull upward to clear his left side for your pin (Step 2).

In an alternative to the previous approach, after lifting his right leg with your shoulder, split his legs as before. Quickly move your left knee up against his haunch in a wedging action (Step 1).

Step 1

Step 2

Now, while your shoulder and your right hand are forcing your opponent to roll slightly to the right, quickly turn your body to the left and pivot your shoulder on his leg, swinging your right leg in a wide arc (Step 2).

After turning more than 90 degrees to the right you will end up in the position shown in Step 3, securing him with Kuzure-Yoko-Shiho—the modified side four-corner pin.

Step 3

Another way of getting past your opponent's leg defense is the pull-up technique. After grabbing both of your opponent's legs at the knees pull your arms inward and upward (Step 1).

Step 1

Move in close enough to grasp his belt on the left and right side of his torso. With this better leverage continue your pushing action, rolling him back until his legs harmlessly paw the air and his shoulders are on the mat (Step 2).

Step 2

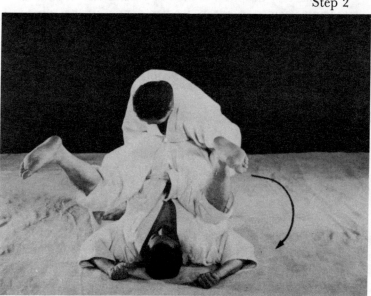

505

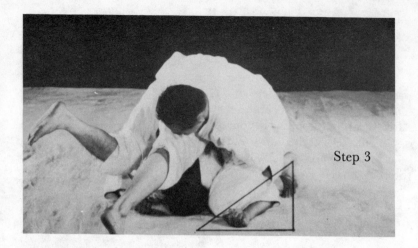

Sweep around to his right side. Pin his right arm with your left leg as shown in Step 3, applying your pin from the side.

Many times—especially during your beginning Judo training, when you'll be wrestling other inexperienced players—your opponent may take defensive action by lying on his stomach. When this occurs quickly move to his side, your body forming a "T" with this position. Slip one hand under his chin and grab his lapel very deep. Slide the other hand underneath his chest, reaching across to grasp his far arm near his elbow. Then place your shoulder against his body and push, at the same time pulling with both hands. Driving with your legs wide apart roll him over on his back. He is then open for Yoko-Shiho-Gatame, the side-locking of the four quarters.

The "T" position

Step 1

In Step 1 is the beginning of a "head on" approach moving to a sideward twisting technique. Grab his belt at the back with your right hand. Hook your left arm under his right armpit, anchoring that hand by grasping your right lapel. Now, twist your opponent to the right. Slide yourself to the left, and with the combined pushing action of your shoulder and pulling motion of your right hand, roll him over on his back (Step 2) and right into Kuzure-Yoko-Shiho, the modified side-locking of the four quarters.

Step 2

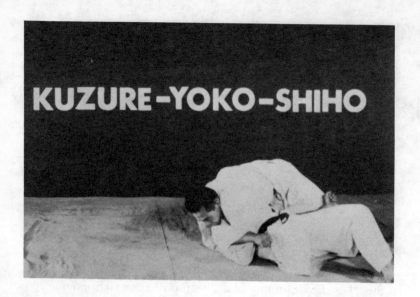

KUZURE-YOKO-SHIHO

When applying this offensive technique, if you encounter particularly stiff resistance to your upward twist (Step 1) you can accomplish your objective in another way. Capitalizing on his resistance, quickly reverse direction downward, rolling to your left in a counter-clockwise movement (Step 2). He will

Step 1

Step 2

roll completely over on his back (Step 3), where you can follow up with Kami-Shiho-Gatame. If your opponent attempts to

Step 3

KAMI-SHIHO-
GATAME

resist your twisting efforts by moving upward, slide your right foot forward between his legs (Step 1). Lean back, as shown in Step 2.

Step 1

Step 2

With your right leg against his left inner thigh (Step 3) flip him directly backwards over your right shoulder (Step 4).

Step 3

You can end on top, and apply Tate-Shiho-Gatame.

Whenever you find yourself on the mat, either thrown by your opponent or missing a throw and falling, immediately face

TATE-SHIHO-GATAME

Step 1

your opponent in the defensive posture shown in Step 1. If your opponent moves to either side, move with him with your legs serving as a barrier against his attack.

As he makes his offensive approach, place your right foot on his left hip (Step 2). At the same time, place your left leg outside of his body, your foot on his right inner thigh. Place your right hand on his left inner lapel and your left hand on his elbow.

Step 2

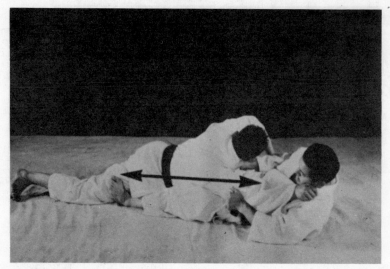

Step 3

Then, by pushing with your feet and pulling with your hands you will stretch him flat on his stomach and stop his forward movement (Step 3).

As he moves forward again, hook your left leg over his right leg as shown in Step 4, and at the same time lock his right forearm against your chest. Now shift your right foot under his

Step 4

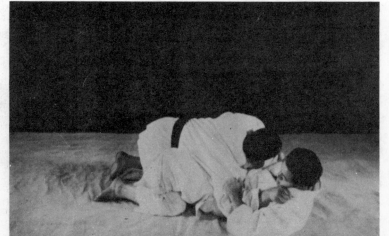

Step 5

left leg and flip him over to the side on his back (Step 5). Then
roll over on top to apply Tate-Shiho-Gatame.

For a variation of the previous technique, reach over and
grasp his belt with your right hand. His right arm is secured
with your left hand. Anchor your arm by holding your own
right lapel (Step 1).

Step 1

Step 2

Your feet are deployed in the same manner as the previous sequence to provide you with a pinning advantage (Step 2).

If your opponent breaks through your defense, you must stop him immediately from making any further progress. This is, accomplished by wrapping your legs around one of his legs as you see in Step 3. Then proceed to free the parts of your body which are confined.

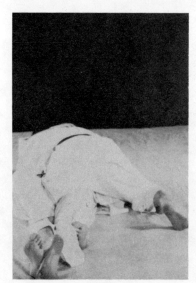

Step 3

A good defense from the opponent's sideward approach is the use of the body bind. When your opponent moves around to your side, roll to your side (Step 1).

Step 1

Lock his encircling arm tightly under your armpit, binding his body to you, and roll to the left (Step 2).

Step 2

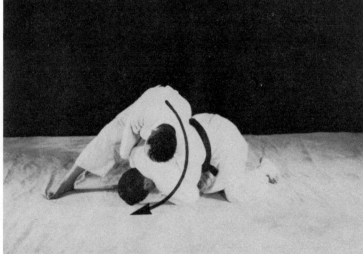

Step 4

Carry him over your back, placing yourself in a favorable position to apply a pin (Steps 3 and 4).

TOMOE-NAGE

Tomoe-Nage, the circle throw, is part of a series of Judo methods known as the sacrifice throws—so-called because you sacrifice your relatively safe standing position, and throw your opponent by going to the mat yourself.

Starting from the right natural posture, push him back as though to break his balance to the rear (Step 1).

As he pushes back to regain his balance, quickly change your left hand from the sleeve to his right lapel and *pull* him well forward and upward on his toes. At the same time, bend your right knee deeply to lower your body and slide your left foot well between his legs (Step 2).

Step 1

Step 2

"O" identifies opponent

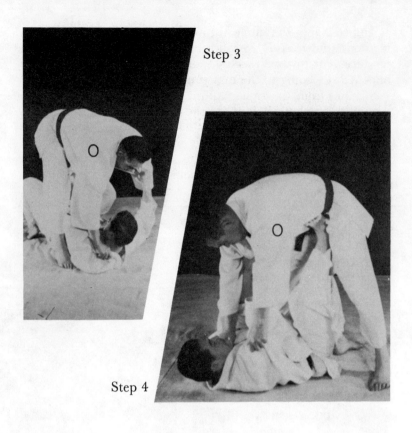

Step 3

Step 4

Roll backwards and slide your body underneath him while continuing to pull in a wide arc with both hands (Step 3). Bring your right foot up so that the sole meets his lower abdomen in the middle of his forward arc. NOTE: It is important that you pull your opponent on to your foot just as he reaches 12 o'clock in his forward circle (Step 4).

O = Opponent

Straightening your knee to provide additional propulsion, add to his toppling momentum by throwing your arms directly backwards with a slight upward pull at the end (Step 5).

Step 5

He will somersault over you and on to the mat in a straight line with your body, as shown in Step 6.

Step 6

SEIRI-UNDO

The purpose of Seiri-Undo or restoration exercise is to bring the body back to normal condition after a strenuous workout. About 2 or 3 minutes is sufficient.

Beginning the exercises

First, lie flat on your stomach in a relaxed manner and have your partner gently pull forward and upward to stretch the muscles.

*Stretching
stomach
muscles*

522

An alternative method is to straddle your partner, gently lift his upper body by grasping his wrists. Raise and lower him several times.

*Straddling
your
partner*

Another method is the back-to-back stretching. When being lifted, remain completely relaxed.

*Stretching
back-to-back*

In the deep-breathing exercises, inhale deeply and slowly as you bring your hands upward. Then exhale slowly as your hands are brought down to your sides.

About to exhale

Now you are probably wondering how to win a Judo match. There are three ways to win.

A forceful throw

IPPON FULL POINT

You can throw your opponent to the mat with such force and skill that you are awarded an "Ippon" or full point by the referee. Such a throw would end the match and you would be awarded the victory.

WAZA-ARI HALF POINT

525

If your throw is not perfect, you are given a "Waza-Ari" or half a point. The match continues until you earn another half point. If the time limit runs out before either opponent earns a full point, the Judoka holding a Waza-Ari is declared the winner.

Pinning opponent

A second way of winning is by a pin. A Judo pin is different from a wrestling pin, since in Judo you do *not* have to hold your opponent's shoulders to the mat. You win by simply controlling your opponent's body with one of the Judo holds for 30 seconds. If you already hold a half point, you need only control him for 25 seconds.

Finally, you can be awarded the match by applying one of the Judo choking holds to your opponent until he concedes.

A Judo choking hold

A throw

A hold

This ends our introduction to Judo. Judo, like any other sport, requires practice and conditioning to achieve the most from your talents. Remember, Judo is more than just a contact sport—it's a physical culture and a philosophy as well. So work hard and practice well. You'll be pleased with the personal rewards you'll gain from Judo, the gentle art.

Moving on the offense

ACKNOWLEDGMENTS

The publishers wish to thank the following individuals and organizations for assistance in the preparation of this volume:

Ira Mandelbaum for taking the photographs in Part I.

Wayne Weissman and Alan Sosnowitz for posing for the photographs in Part I.

Voit, a subsidiary of American Machine and Foundry, for photographs of the exercise equipment shown on pages 14, 15, 17, 19, 22 and 24.

Dale S. Cunningham and Paul Kuttner for translation of Part II, and Falken-Verlag Erich Sicker, the original German publisher.

Terumasa Arai, instructor of the Goshindo Kempo Association, for assisting; Lynn Klein, Ray Lennon and Robert Sjolin for posing; and William Greaves for taking photographs for Part III.

Recreation Films and Dallas Jones for the photographs for Part IV.

Index